Liberation

Francisco Candido Xavier

Liberation

By the Spirit
Andre Luiz

Translated by: Darrel W. Kimble and Marcia M. Saiz

Copyright © 2013 by
BRAZILIAN SPIRITIST FEDERATION
Av. L 2 Norte – Q. 603 – Conjunto F (SGAN)
70830-030 – Brasilia (DF) – Brazil

ISBN 978-1-936547-97-5

Original title in Portuguese:
LIBERTAÇÃO
Brazil, 1949

Translated by: Darrel W. Kimble and Marcia M. Saiz
Cover design by: Evelin Yuri Furuta and Luciano Carneiro Holanda
Photo: www.istockphoto.com/ galdzer

Edition of
EDICEI OF AMERICA
8425 Biscayne Blvd. - Suite 104
Miami, FL 33138 USA
www.ediceiofamerica.com
info@ediceiofamerica.com
Phone: (305) 758-7444
Fax: (305) 758-7449

First Edition 7/2013

Authorized edition by Brazilian Spiritist Federation

INTERNATIONAL DATA FOR CATALOGING IN PUBLICATION (ICP)

L979   Luiz, Andre (Spirit).
             Liberation / dictated by the spirit Andre Luiz ; [received by] Francisco
         Candido Xavier ; translated by Darrel W. Kimble and Marcia M. Saiz. – Miami
         (FL), USA : Edicei of America, 2013.
             264 p. ; 21 cm

             Original title: Libertação
             ISBN 978-1-936547-97-5

             1. Spiritualism. 2. Spirit writings. I. Xavier, Francisco Candido, 1910-
         2002. II. Title.

                                          CDD 133.9
                                          CDU 133.7

Contents

AT THE OPEN GATES

At the open entrance gates to the Christian endeavor and edifying knowledge that Andre Luiz is disclosing to us, we are pleased to recall an ancient Egyptian tale about a little red fish.

In the middle of a beautiful yard, there was a large pond lined with turquoise-blue tiles.

The pond was fed by a small stone canal, and its waters exited through a narrow grated opening at the opposite end.

In this welcoming pond lived a large community of fish, lolling about, well-fed and content, in intricate hiding places that were luxuriant and shady. These fish had elected one of their finned comrades to act as their king, and there they lived, completely unconcerned amidst gluttony and idleness.

Amongst them, however, lived a little red fish who was bullied by all the others.

He wasn't allowed to look for even the smallest worm or find shelter in one of the muddy crooks and crannies.

Being voracious and pot-bellied, the other fish hogged the best worms for themselves and they indifferently occupied all the places meant for rest.

The little red fish swam and suffered. He moved about constantly, persecuted by the heat or tormented by hunger.

Since he couldn't find a spot in which to rest in his vast home, the little fish didn't have much time for leisure, so he began to take quite an interest in studying the pond.

He counted all the tiles that lined the sides of the pond; he made a list of all the crannies and caves, and he knew exactly where most of the mud would accumulate as a result of downpours.

After a long time and much investigation, he discovered the barred drain.

Faced with an unforeseen opportunity for a world of healthy adventure, he said to himself:

"Wouldn't it be interesting to get to know life better and explore other places?"

He decided to leave.

In spite of the fact that he was so skinny from lack of nourishment, he still suffered terribly when he lost several scales as he swam through the very narrow passageway.

Saying encouraging promises to himself, he advanced optimistically along the canal, enchanted with the new scenery rich with flowers and sunlight, and he continued on, inebriated with hope.

After a while, the red fish reached a big river and made a lot of new acquaintances.

He met fish from many different families who befriended him, advising him about the problems he might run into along the way and pointing out the easiest course.

He was astonished to see humans and animals on the banks, boats and bridges, and in palaces and vehicles, cottages and woodlands.

Since he was used to having little, he lived very frugally, thus never losing his lightness and natural agility.

At last, the red fish reached the ocean, swooning from the newness and thirsting for exploration.

To start with, enraptured by his passion for observation, he approached a big whale for whom all the water of the pond in which he had lived would be nothing but a small sip. Impressed with this spectacle, he came closer than he should have and was sucked in along with the elements that made up the whale's first meal of the day.

In such a fix, the little fish prayed to the Fish God, asking for protection in the belly of the monster, and in spite of the darkness, from which he asked to be saved, his prayer was answered, because the mighty cetacean began to heave and vomit, returning the little fish to the ocean's currents.

The thankful and happy little traveler went in search of empathetic friends and he learned to avoid other dangers and temptations.

Completely transformed in his concepts of the world, he began to enjoy the infinite riches of life. He came across luminous plants, strange animals, gliding stars, and a variety of flowers in the ocean depths. But best of all, he found many thin and studious little fish like himself, with whom he felt wonderfully content.

He was now living smilingly and peacefully with hundreds of friends in the Palace of Coral that he had chosen as a delightful home. Looking back on his troublesome beginning, he realized that aquatic creatures could be more fully protected only in the sea, because when summer became unbearably hot, waters from higher altitudes would continue to flow into the ocean.

The little fish thought and thought… and feeling an immense compassion for those with whom he had lived his early years, he decided to dedicate himself to their progress and salvation.

Wouldn't it be fitting to return and tell them about the truth? Wouldn't it be praiseworthy to assist them by giving them this precious bit of information?

The red fish didn't hesitate.

Supported by the generosity of the friendly benefactors who lived with him in the Palace of Coral, he undertook the long trip back.

He returned to the river; from the river he went up creeks and from the creeks, he swam up the canal that led him back to his first home.

Sleek and satisfied as ever because of the life of study and service to which he had dedicated himself, he passed through the barred opening and anxiously went looking for his old companions.

Stimulated by this exploit of love, the red fish believed that his return would cause both surprise and general enthusiasm. The entire community would surely celebrate his feat. But he soon learned that no one cared in the least.

They were the same fat lazy fish as always, lolling about in the same mud-filled crannies protected by lotus flowers, from which they emerged only to munch on larvae, flies or poor little worms.

He cried out that he had come home, but no one paid him any mind, because none of them had even noticed his absence in the first place.

Receiving only ridicule, he then sought out the fish king, a fish with enormous gills, and told him about his revealing adventure.

The king, somewhat benumbed in his hunger for power, gathered all the other fish and allowed the little messenger to explain himself.

Their despised benefactor took advantage of this opportunity and enthusiastically explained that there was another glorious and endless liquid world beyond the pond. The pond was nothing and could disappear at any time. Beyond the nearby drain another life and another experience unfolded. Outside it, there were creeks decorated with flowers, mighty rivers full of all kinds of beings, and finally, the ocean, where life appeared richer and more surprising each day. He described the life of the mullet and salmon, the trout and the dogfish. He told them about the sunfish, the rabbit fish and the buckler dory. He told them that he had seen the sky adorned with millions of sublime stars and that he had discovered giant trees, huge ships, ocean-side cities, fearsome monsters, submerged gardens and starfish. He even offered to lead them to his Palace of Coral, where they could all live peacefully and prosperously. Finally, he informed them that such happiness, however, had its price. They would all have to lose a lot of weight, which meant abstaining from so many worms and larvae in their dark hideaways, and they would have to learn to work and study as much as required for the venturesome journey.

When he was done, his listeners guffawed loudly.

Nobody believed the little fish.

A few speakers took the floor, solemnly stating that the little red fish was clearly delirious; that any other life outside the pond was obviously impossible; that his story about creeks, rivers and oceans was the mere fantasy of a deranged mind. Others even declared that they were speaking in the name of the Fish God, who looked down upon them and them only.

Just to ridicule the little fish a little more, the king went with him to the drain, but after making a half-hearted attempt to go through it, the king exclaimed loudly:

"Can't you see that not even one of my fins would fit through here? You big fool!" Get out of here! Don't disturb our peace of mind. Our pond is the center of the universe... no one else has a life like ours!"

Expelled by these blows of sarcasm, the little fish made the trip back and permanently settled in the Palace of Coral, biding his time.

Some years later, a terrible draught devastated the land.

Water levels dropped; the pond where those idle and vain fish lived went dry, and the whole community perished, stranded in the mud.

***

Andre Luiz's efforts to light a torch in the darkness is like the little red fish's mission.

Enchanted by his discoveries involving the infinite way, accomplished after much suffering and conflict, he returns to the environs of the earth's surface to tell his former companions that beyond the little cubicles where they live, another life shines, more beautiful and intense, but which requires detailed individual improvement for the journey through the narrow passageway, which gives access to sublime enlightenment.

Andre speaks, informs, prepares, enlightens…

However, there are many "human fish" who smile and live amid mordancy and indifference in their search for transitory crannies, in their struggle for temporary larvae.

They expect to find a cost-free heaven after death, full of dazzling wonders.

But aside from Andre Luiz and us – humble servants of goodwill – the Divine Shepherd spoke these imperishable words to all those walking the pathway of human life: "To each according to his deeds."

Emmanuel
Pedro Leopoldo, February 22, 1949

1
Listening to Explanations

We were gathered in the large auditorium of an educational institution. Minister Flacus was gazing at us with a look saturated with pleasant magnetism that invited us to ponder what he was saying.

A few dozen colleagues and I had assembled there to listen to his edifying lecture, and there was no doubt that it was proving to be of profound interest.

We were free to ask questions at any time concerning the subject at hand and use any information that might be relevant to the new endeavor that we were about to undertake.

For a long time I had heard comments alluding to purgatorial colonies that were fully organized for the expiatory work for which they were intended, bringing together thousands of individuals rooted in wrongdoing. Instructor Gubio, who was sitting silently beside us, had finally given us permission to accompany him to one such huge colony.

Interested in the speaker's fluent and gripping lecture, we followed the course of his thoughts with the understandable expectation of pupils who do not want to miss one bit of what was being taught. Serenity and attention transpired on all our faces. Each one of us there in that auditorium was a candidate for assisting ignorant brothers and sisters being tormented in darkness...

Commanding our full attention, the Minister continued, confidently:

"Superiors wanting to engage in persistent and substantial work on behalf of inferiors cannot use the same weapons as inferiors use. If they do, they will be lowering themselves to their level. Strictness belongs to those who teach, but love is the companion of those who serve.

"We know that most of the time education moves from the periphery to the center, but the truly perfecting work of inner renewal does the opposite. Both learning and inner renewal, however, are nourished and controlled by the almost unknown powers of the mind.

"The human mind deals with both mental power and electricity, but with the difference that, although it has learned to control the latter in the ongoing transformation of the earth, it is barely aware of the former, which, nonetheless, presides over our every activity in life.

"So, strictly speaking, there are no infernal realms according to the old theological model, realms that are inhabited forever by evil spirits of all eras; instead, there are spheres of darkness where consciences dulled in ignorance gather, crystallized in condemnable idleness or confused in the temporary eclipse of their reason. Desperate and rebellious, they have created regions of reparatory torment. Such individuals cannot be regenerated using the power of words alone, however. They need the effective kind of assistance that can alter their inner vibrational tenor, thus raising their level of feeling and thinking.

"Eminent thinkers have mapped out instructions for the salvation of souls, but we are of the opinion that there are more than enough such scripts in all areas of terrestrial knowledge regarding the matter. What we need now are individuals who can guide human thought towards the Higher Realms. To undertake this endeavor while stimulated only by cultural values would be to consecrate technocracy, which seeks to merely mechanize life, thus destroying its glorious seeds of improvisation, perpetuity and eternity.

"There has never been a lack of great politicians and venerable leaders.

"They pass through the crowds, stirring them up or forming them into regiments. But we must bear in mind that human organization by itself cannot meet the needs of the eternal being.

"Pericles, the statesman who bequeathed his name to a century, accomplishes constructive educational work with the Greeks; even so, he does not lessen their bellicosity and their lust for supremacy. Consequently, he succumbs to the assault of terrible grief.

"Alexander the Great organizes a vast empire, establishing a remarkable civilization; nonetheless, he cannot keep his generals from pursuing bloody conflicts, spreading plunder and death.

"Augustus the Divine unifies the Roman Empire on solid foundations, establishing an advanced political program on behalf of all, but he cannot manage to banish from Rome the madness for domination at any price.

"Constantine the Great, advocate of the defenseless Christians, offers a new standard of life to the planet; nevertheless, he fails to change the detestable attitude of those who wage war in God's name.

"Napoleon, the dictator, establishes new methods of material progress over all the earth, but he himself is trapped in the claws of tyranny because of his greed.   "Pasteur, the scientist, defends the health of the human body, devoting himself selflessly to silently combating the microbial jungle; however, he cannot keep his contemporaries from mutually ruining each other in ruthless and inexplicable competition.

"We are faced with a world that looks civilized on its surface, a world that clamors not only for those who teach the Good, but especially for those who actually practice it.

"It is absolutely essential that the torrents of compassion from heaven fall upon the fountainheads of culture in the valleys of the earth by way of the mountains of love and self-denial.

"Christ not only shines because of his sublime teachings, but because of his exemplary life as well. In following him, we must have the courage to assist and save others by descending into the recesses of the abyss.

"Not far from this place of relative peace, millions of beings are living in dark realms of disillusionment and despair, crying out for compassion… Why not turn on a pious light in the night in which they are immersed without guidance? Why not sow hope in the hearts of those who have lost faith in themselves?

"Thus, faced with huge collectivities sorrowfully pleading for readjustment, healing assistance cannot wait.

"We are spirits that are still too infinitely humble and imperfect to suddenly apply as candidates for angelhood.

"Compared to the unfathomable grandeur of millions of suns that obey the divine and sovereign laws throughout the universe, our earth, with all the realms of ultra-physical substance surrounding it, is like a tiny orange compared to the Himalayas.

And if we compare ourselves to the sublimity of the high order spirits that govern in wisdom and holiness, we are no more than bacteria controlled by the impulse of hunger and the magnetism of love. Nonetheless, raised to the simple heights of intelligence, we are microbes who dream about never-ending self-growth.

"While human beings – our brothers and sisters – split the atom in awe, we, as spirits outside the dense body, study this same energy from aspects that earthly science, for now, can barely imagine. As travelers of infinite progress, we are just beginning to probe the mental power that conditions the manifestations in the most varied planes of nature.

"Still imprisoned by the law of return, we have accomplished multi-secular recapitulations for many millennia.

"We know today that the human spirit, taken as a whole, has had the ability to reason for exactly forty thousand years … Nonetheless, with the same furious impetus with which Neanderthals killed one another with hatchet blows, humans of modern times – regarded as the glorious era of world powers – exterminate their brothers and sisters with firearms.

"Commentators lightly endowed with religious principles regard this sinister anomaly as being merely the obstinacy of imperfect, frail flesh, as if the flesh were a permanent diabolical persona; however, they overlook the fact that this dense matter is only the complex whole of countless inferior lives undergoing the process of improvement, growth and liberation.

"Down on the earth, the mind functions as if it has been sedated by the dangerous narcotics of illusion; however, we will help it sense and realize that the spirit continues vibrating on all angles of existence.

"Each species of being, from the crystal to the human, and from the human to the angel, encompasses countless families of creatures operating on a specific frequency of the universe. And divine love reaches all of them, like the sunlight that embraces the sage and the worm.

"However, those who advance to a higher sphere remain connected to those in the next one down.

"The plant kingdom resorts to the mineral realm to support itself and evolve. Animals use plants in their work of improvement. Humans assist each other to grow mentally and move ahead...

"The kingdoms of life, that is, the kingdoms known on earth, torment each other.

"They torture and devour one another so that spiritual qualities may develop and shine, reflecting the divine light..."

The learned Minister took a long pause, gave us a kindly look and continued:

"But... beyond the human condition, beyond the sensorial boundaries that contain the incarnate soul, carefully protecting it with limited sight and the beneficent forgetfulness of its past, a vast spiritual empire begins: humankind's neighboring world. There, millions of imperfect spirits move about, sharing with earth's creatures the habitable conditions of the planet's surface. Human beings situated on a different vibrational wavelength lean on the incarnate mind by means of countless phalanxes of creatures that are as semiconscious of responsibility and as incomplete in virtue as humans themselves.

"Bringing together millions of embryonic lives, matter is a condensation of energy, serving the imperatives of the 'self' which presides over its destiny.

"From hydrogen to more complex atomic units, the power of the eternal spirit acts as the guiding lever for protons, neutrons and electrons along the infinite road of life. The embodied intelligence lingers in the human sphere in a transitory region suited to its needs for progress and perfection, in which protoplasm gives it the tools it needs for work, growth and expansion. Nevertheless, within this same space, matter extends itself to assume other states, where the discarnate mind, on its journey to acquire knowledge and virtue, is rooted in the physical sphere, seeking to dominate and absorb it, establishing a gigantic struggle of thought unfathomable to ordinary humans.

"Frustrated in their aspirations of vain dominion in their heavenly dwelling, men and women from all climes and civilizations meet up and collide after death in this region, where their earthly activities continue as usual, choosing the instinct of ruling over the earth as the only happiness worth achieving. Due to the permanent discord reigning among them, these rebellious children of Providence try to discredit the divine grandeur, thereby stimulating the autocratic power of their proud and rebellious intelligence. They seek to use their earthly activities for the unlimited expansion of hatred and rebelliousness, of vanity and criminality, as if the planet, in its lower expression, were the only paradise that has not yet completely submitted to their whims. Encased in their own ignorance where fear and viciousness, distress and reciprocal persecution destroy their strength and waste their time, they do not realize how bad their situation really is.

"Apart from true love, every union is temporary, and war will always be the natural state of those who persist in rebelliousness.

"A divided and tormented spiritual kingdom surrounds the human experience in all directions, and its purpose is to enlarge the permanent realm of tyranny and power.

"We know that the sun functions by emitting radiations that maternally nourish life millions of kilometers away. Notwithstanding the conditions of matter in which we are immersed, we need to remember that the most rudimentary existences in our system, from the illuminated peaks to the deepest caves, are subject to its influence.

"As is the case with the gigantic bodies of the cosmos, spiritually speaking we too are on our way to the culmination of evolution, experiencing each other's radiations. In this multifarious process of interchange, attraction, magnetization and repulsion, worlds and souls improve themselves in the universal community.

"Within this reality, our earthly activity takes place in a field of influences that not even we, human learners in the higher realms, can grasp for the time being.

"Incapable of going straight from the grave to heaven, the children of despair organize themselves into vast colonies of hate and moral misery, fighting amongst themselves for control of the earth. Like us, they possess a large, invaluable intellectual patrimony and, as fallen angels of Science, they seek, above all, the debasement of the divine processes that guide planetary evolution.

"Entrenched in the dark passions that flog their consciences, spirits whose minds are crystallized in rebelliousness try in vain to undermine the Divine Harmony, creating cysts of inferior life on the earth. They know countless ways to disturb, hurt, obscure and destroy. They enslave the beneficent service of reincarnation in great expiatory sectors and make use of agents of discord against every embodiment of sublime purposes for which God designed our actions.

"Men and women, who, in moments of semi-liberation from their bodies, managed to perceive the existence of these rebellious spirits, dashed back to their bodies, frightened by the horrible sight, and spread the idea of a punitive and never-ending hell set in sinister regions beyond death.

"Drawing on traditional theology, the child-like mind, animated by Providence's paternal tenderness, could never grasp the true essence of the spiritual reality that governs our destinies.

"Few understand that death is just a modification of one's body and fewer still are those – even the most learned religious individuals – who are wise enough to live in the physical vessel according to the superior principles they have espoused. We have come to a time when we must proclaim the old truths to old ears and new truths to the new ears of the world's youthful intelligence.

"As presumptive heir to the heavenly crown, human beings are their own guides on the long stretches of the evolutionary road. Between those spirits who are close to the angelic state and the primitives who are still limited by irrationality there are thousands of different levels occupied by reason and sentiment of the most varied nuances. And if there is a bright and wonderful tide of discarnate and incarnate spirits that are on their way to the mount of spiritual sublimation while singing a glorious hymn of work, immortality, beauty and hope in praise of life, there is another tide, a dark and miserable one, that wants to descend into the den of spiritual darkness, spreading trouble, discouragement, disorder and shadow, and paying tribute to death.

"Imperfect spirits that we still are, we follow those with whom we are attuned and we either reap the rewards of ascent and victory, or the damages of descent and failure, controlled as we are by intelligences that are stronger than ours and who stay at our side in the progressive or depressive zone in which we have put ourselves.

"Hell, then, is a matter of spiritual direction.

"Satan is the perverse intelligence.

"Evil represents a waste of time or the use of one's energy contrary to the Lord's designs.

"Suffering means reparation or a renewing lesson.

"Fallen souls, however, no matter who they are, do not comprise a spiritual race sentenced to languish in a demonic state of madness forever as part of the discarnate collectivity, in a completely senseless condition. No, they comingle with the terrestrial multitudes and have a strong influence on many homes and administrations. The fundamental interest of the most intelligent ones is to keep the world distracted and in the dark by encouraging ignorance and selfishness, postponing indefinitely the arrival of the Kingdom of God among humankind.

"The regions of darkness they inhabit undergo considerable changes over the millennia, in the same way as the provisory regions inhabited by earth's various peoples. The matter comprising these regions of darkness undergoes tremendous modifications and, according to the molds of the Infinite Good, a wonderful process of natural selection takes place as part of this transformation. Nevertheless, despite the fact that these regions are constantly renewed with replacements, their inhabitants remain where they have been for centuries, watching the course of civilizations and closely following their magnificence and their experiences, as well as their afflictions and defeats."

When the Minister paused for a moment to give members of the audience the chance to ask questions – something that seemed to me to be opportune and intentional – one of them asked:

"Esteemed benefactor, we know what you are saying is true; but why doesn't the wise and compassionate Lord just eliminate such an awful state of things?"

The learned mentor nodded in understanding and replied:

"Isn't that like asking why it is taking so long for us to live according to the Divine Kingdom? Do you believe you are so enlightened that you can deny the dark side of your own personality? Have you rid yourself of all the temptations that flow from the mysterious inner recesses of your inner struggle? Don't you realize that the earth itself has circles of light and darkness, as do the recesses of our own hearts? Just as we do battle amid formidable inner conflicts, so does planetary life in its innermost folds. As for the Lord's intervention, let us remember that our current studies are not concerned with aspects of compassion, but with matters of justice.

"Together – discarnate and incarnate humanity – we represent only a minute portion of the universal family, confined as we are to our unique vibrational frequency.

"We are merely a few billion beings faced with Eternity. Let's not forget that just as it takes a diamond to cut and polish another diamond, evil can only be corrected by evil, meaning that justice works through apparent injustice until love is born and redeems those that have condemned themselves to long and painful sentences before the Good Law.

"Perverse, calculating, criminal and inconsequent individuals are watched over by spirits of the same nature, ones that are attuned to their own tendencies.

"Actually, since guardian spirits never neglect their wards, there has never been a lack of heaven's protection against the torments that evil-hardened souls have sown on earth; even so, it would be highly illogical to assign an angel to watch over criminals.

"Generally speaking, incarnate spirits are surrounded by the somber and debasing radiations from imperfect and indecisive spirits like themselves, spirits that may be invisible to them but share their homes with them, nonetheless.

"Thus, the planet is nothing more than a huge labyrinth for spiritual growth, and only those individuals that have grown to an exceptional degree through their own efforts manage to escape to the sublime spheres.

"Regarding a similar situation, the Divine Master stated before the judge in Jerusalem: *"My kingdom is not of this world"* and, for the same reason, Paul of Tarsus, after anguishing struggles, wrote to the Ephesians: *For our struggle is not against flesh and blood, but against the rulers, against the authorities, against the powers of this dark world, and against the spiritual forces of evil in the heavenly realms.*

"Therefore, just beyond the human kingdom, the immense empire of discarnate intelligences unceasingly takes part in humanity's judgment.

"Understanding our condition as imperfect workers who hold on to old problems and terrible inhibitions that keep us from growing towards the light, we should develop resources that will help us, recognizing the fact that the redemptive endeavor is educative work par excellence.

"The sacrifice of the Master was the Divine yeast leavening the whole loaf. That is why, above all, Jesus is the Donor of Sublimation for life eternal. He abstained from manipulating the passion of the crowds, because he knew that the true work of salvation is rooted in the heart. He kept his distance from political decrees, in spite of his reverence and unquestionable respect for the established authority, knowing that working for the Heavenly Kingdom does not depend on outward commitments but on individualism that is attuned to goodwill and the spirit of self-denial on behalf of others.

"Without our personal cooperation in the work of the Good, the regenerative endeavor will lag indefinitely. It is imperative that we extend our fraternal assistance to those temporarily numbed in evil, so that they may accept the Divine Will and learn to use the power of their inner light. Only love that is felt, believed in and lived by us can bring about an eclosion of love in our neighbors. If we do not focus the energies of the soul on what is divine and adjust their magnetism to the Center of the Universe, any redemptive plan is merely a bunch of words and thus blatantly impossible."

The Minister ended his lecture with a question:

"Have I made myself clear?"

We were all eager to hear more; however, Flacus, surrounded by a luminous aura, came down from the podium and started chatting with us.

The lecture was over.

As always, what I had just heard piqued my interest, but I had to await the right opportunity to come along to get fuller explanations.

2
A Conversation with
the Instructor

When we left the educational establishment, Instructor Gubio looked at Eloi, our companion, and at me with his lucid eyes and said:

"It's hard for a lot of people to understand the intelligent regimentation of evil spirits. Nevertheless, it's logical and natural. If we are still a long ways from holiness in spite of the lofty purposes that have been guiding us, what can be said about miserable brothers and sisters who have willingly let themselves be caught in the web of ignorance and wickedness? They haven't grasped the fact that there is a region that is higher than the physical sphere, to which they are still bound by strong ties. Since they are entangled in forces of a low vibrational level, they cannot grasp the beauty of the higher life, and as fragile, sick mentalities bow down in humiliation, the spirits of impiety impose their rule on them. They organize them into large communities and guide them on the dark foundations of hatred and quiet desperation. They organize veritable cities that house huge phalanxes of souls, who, ashamed of themselves, flee before any manifestation of the divine light. Children of rebellion and darkness gather there by the thousands, seeking self-preservation and supporting one another."

Perceiving our obvious surprise, the Instructor continued in response to our inner inquiries.

"Such troubled colonies must have started when the first earthly intelligences began indulging in disobedience and rebelliousness before the decrees of the Heavenly Paternity. The soul that has fallen into unharmonious vibrations by abusing the freedom that was entrusted to it must weave the threads of its own readjustment. But millions of our lazy, impenitent brothers and sisters refuse to undertake such an endeavor, prolonging the maze in which they often remain lost for centuries. They are incapable of making the urgent journey to heaven because of the destructive passions that magnetize them, and in accordance with the inferior tendencies they have in common, they band together close to the earth's surface, whose inferior emanations and lives continue to nourish them in the same way that it nourishes incarnates. The main objective of these dark armies is to conserve the mental backwardness of the human being so that the planet will remain under their tyrannical yoke as much as possible."

Gubio's comments seared my mind.

I, myself, had spent time in the lower realms of life after corporeal death[1]; however, I had never come across such organized condensations of evil entities in the spirit realm, although I did hear astonishing references to them on several occasions.

---

1   An account of this may be found in the book *Nosso Lar* by the Spirit Author. – Tr.

In fact, I had not been able to rid myself of all my memories of that awful time that the door of the grave had opened to me.

I remembered having been pursued across large marshy areas … Tormented and wretched, I had wandered in misery for what seemed like days and nights on end. Nevertheless, I could not grasp the fact that evil activities had some sort of guiding organism. Consequently, with my mind now focused on the aims of the Good, I ventured to ask:

"After death, and divested of their heavy garment of flesh, why can't such backward legions see, better than ever, that they are fighting a battle that they can never win? Transported to the plane of pure enlightenment, can't they grasp their situation? Aren't they surrounded by the most sublime revelations of nature? Don't they realize how much better edifying and worthwhile study would be in the lofty aspiration of attaining sanctifying knowledge? Why do they congregate like that in despicable and diabolical crowds? It is easy to understand that the evolutionary journey of the human being continues after the grave, but deliberately postponing it due to cruelty and hatred would baffle any mind."

The guide smiled politely and explained:

"We are talking about spirits who are perfectly human, in spite of being discarnate, and such questions, Andre, may even be asked regarding the physical realm. Before awakening our consciousness to divine revelation, why did we ourselves stay bound to the lower spheres every day, transgressing the Law so spectacularly? After all, the blessed flood of sunlight pouring down incessantly from Infinite Space was right there in front of us … We knew that the existence of our body would be brief; that we would have to face death like everyone else; that we would have to return from the physical world through the same mysterious doorway we had used when we entered it. Even so, how many times did we disdain the Sublime Wisdom with our attitude of criminal indifference? In light of the suggestions from the Divine Plane that now inhabit your mind, do you recall any time in the past when you truly thought about your own sublimation? If we unearth our past, my dear fellow, we will uncover deplorable memories ... But we must neither stop nor get discouraged. Like the fragile shoot, we must grow by reaching for the air above us, and in spite of the shackles that bind us, just like the humble tree that is bound to the remains of the complex envelope that used to contain its seed, we must rise to the pure air and broadness of conditions so that we may produce the Good the Lord expects from us."

Gubio's arguments were wonderful and suggestive, but I still had problems accepting the idea of managed purgatories and hells.

"I agree with what you're saying," I said respectfully, "but such ignorance that keeps us deluded beyond the body is almost incredible ... The grave opens a new pathway to all of us. It is reasonable that the troubled mind must endure the pain of readjustment until it recovers; but a discarnate spirit taking control of certain sections of that pathway as if it were their absolute master in order to continue its tyranny is something that I just can't grasp."

"Yes," replied the guide convincingly, "for someone who has thought long and hard about the subject, but in a way that is contrary to reality, the idea is quite surprising; however, I see no obstacles to grasping the lesson. For example, we know that ordinary human beings went through the evolutionary stage of irrationality thousands of years ago, yet on many occasions they still display behavior that is beneath them."

Impressing a grave tone on his pleasant and fraternal voice, he added:

"We must bear in mind that we discarnates live in a field of matter characterized by a specific, though rarefied, density, when compared to our old physical forms, and that our mind, whether we are on the earth or here, is a psychic center of attraction and repulsion. The incarnate spirit lives in a zone of slower vibrations, confined to a vehicle made up of trillions of cells that are microscopic lives in and of themselves. Each life, however, no matter how insignificant, possesses a special magnetic quality. In spite of being conditioned by cosmic and moral laws, the will controls the community of living corpuscles that serve it for a limited time, much like the electrician who connects the power coming from the substation for activities in a swamp or a tower. Since each of us is an intelligent power holding creative faculties and acting within the universe, we are continuously generating psychological agents through mental energy, which exteriorizes our thoughts, and with it we create positive causes, whose effects may be near or far from their point of origin. If we choose not to use our will, we will invariably be pawns of the predominant circumstances surrounding us, but as soon as we do choose to use it, we must resolve the problem of directing it, because our personal states reflect our inner choices. There are principles, forces and laws in the microcosmic universe as well as in the macrocosmic one. If someone directs his or her will toward the idea of sickness and disease, it will respond to the appeal with all the characteristics of the patterns structured by the diseased thought, since a mental suggestion instills affinity and receptivity in the organic region according to the impulse. And in obedience to inner orders repeatedly received, the microbes that live and reproduce in the mental fields of the millions of persons who nurture them will then rush en masse into the cells that attract them, forming in the body the visualized infirmity. Of course, with regard to this matter, there is the issue of necessary trials involving cases in which each individual is reborn in answer to the demands of expiatory lessons; but even then, the problem of mental connection is infinitely important because the sick person who takes pleasure in the acceptance and praise of his or her decadence ends up as an excellent incubator of bacteria and morbid symptoms. On the other hand, when the spirit undergoing readjustment fights bravely against the ill, even if it is beneficial and deserved, it finds plentiful resources to focus on the Good and to enter the stream of life victorious."

I was following his explanations and was profoundly edified, and in spite of a lengthy, spontaneous pause, I did not dare interrupt the course of his argument so as not to break his line of reasoning.

The esteemed and worthy Gubio continued:

"Our mind is an entity placed between superior and inferior forces, and its goal is spiritual perfection. Our perispirit – the sublime result of evolution – as well as our physical body, may be compared to the poles of an electro-magnetic device. The incarnate spirit experiences inferior influences through the areas of the sex organs and abdomen, and receives superior stimuli – even if they come from non-sublimated souls – through the heart and brain. When individuals seek to gain control of their will, they choose the company they prefer and set out on the pathway they desire. The lower spheres may be home to millions of primitive influences – even beneath earthy forms – urging us to hold on to emotions and desires and equipping us for momentous falls into the abysses of destructive sentiment – through which we already journeyed many centuries ago – but there are also millions of sanctifying appeals inviting us to ascend towards glorious immortality."

The Instructor set his piercing and peaceful gaze on us and asked:

"Now do you understand why some spirits choose the dark house of wrongdoing after the grave, just as there are millions of incarnate spirits, who, in full harmony with their earthly nature, love to live in the house of infirmity? Entrenched mental attitudes are not easily changed. When unwilling to abide by the sanctifying principles of the idealistic terrain so that they may inwardly nourish themselves with the task to which they are committed, monarchs who rules over thousands, leaders who are used to imposing iron-fisted decrees, or persons who are used to others submitting to them do not become humble servants overnight just because they have rid themselves of the burden of their physical cells. If they are not sent to the abysses of insanity in the total eclipse of their reason for an indeterminable length of time due to their misuse of their intellect and power, they are retained and respected in the evolutionary endeavor of the world as a result of the appreciable and worthy qualities they have already gained – although violent passions still characterize their inner life – and they are utilized by higher order spirits in the work of perfecting the planet. Thus, they monitor and readjust the weaker and, in turn, they are monitored and readjusted by the stronger, gradually and imperceptibly converting to the Supreme Good and accepting the Divine Plan, whose execution they take part in with faithfulness and valor. In such a position, they help and are helped, they give and receive, driving progress and progressing in turn."

He paused briefly, and then continued in another direction:

"Such a reality compels us to ponder the extent of spiritual work from every evolutionary angle. Education for life eternal is not limited to the superficial learning that an ordinary person receives after a few years at a university. It is a work of patience that requires centuries. If there are trees that live for hundreds of years to accomplish their purposes, what can be said about the millennia required by one individual for his or her own sublimation?

"Thus, we mustn't forget the love we owe to the ignorant, the weak and the unfortunate. We must walk in the footsteps of those who once extended their compassionate hands to us."

The argument was too constructive for us to interrupt with more questions.

Gubio took advantage of the chance to explain further:

"The atoms comprising the Eucharistic host in a church are essentially the same as those comprising the lowly bread in a penitentiary. Hence, all matter per se is passive and pliable, and is the same whether in the hands of the learned or the ignorant, in the hands of loving entities or brutes, in the condensed state known on the earth or in states known elsewhere. Consequently, we can understand the transitory forms constructed on our plane by individuals who have turned from the Good. For those who anesthetized their faculties in the pursuit of fleeting pleasures, a long and painful process of incomprehension follows the separation from the flesh. Considering the fact that most people pursue the sensations of the physical body – as if the genetic attractions and the frenetic attachment to temporary assets of the lowest circles made up their entire happiness in the world – the reaping of imbalanced personalities is always disquieting because it keeps unaltered the dark ranks of the insensate cultivators of selfish happiness at any price. Dangerous lunatics who are willingly controlled by sovereign intelligences specializing in domination make up dreadful hoards that guard the exits from the lower realms on all sides."

"Why does God allow such an anomaly?" asked Eloi with obvious consternation. "Wouldn't a mere order from the Eternal One be enough to cleanse the disharmony?"

The helpful Gubio did not make him wait for an answer.

Smiling openly, he replied enthusiastically:

"Isn't that like asking why the Lord has waited for us this long? Why we believe in wondrous paradises? Don't we know that each person will either sit on the throne that he or she has crafted or will plunge into the depths of the abyss that he or she wanted? Moreover, we must remember that if the stonecutter uses a rough file to polish the stone, the Lord of the Universe uses hardened hearts, temporarily alienated from His Work, to perfect the character of the children who have wandered away from His Home. The best judge cannot always be the nicest individual.

"Moral qualities and superior virtues are not mere talk – they are living forces, without which the human spirit cannot evolve. Ordinary people are addicted to the safeguards of external resources and they focus their best sentiments on them, thereby hanging on to useless fantasies ... They consequently imprison their minds in insecurity, fragility and fear. The shock of death impresses tremendous conflicts on their perispiritual organism, the vehicle intended for their manifestation in the new circle of matter that is different than what they were used to; and after they wasted blessed years in the didactic field of the corporeal realm entangled in deplorable conflicts, they roam about, afflicted, lifeless and rebellious, and join the first group of wicked spirits that can promise them the continuation of a life of fictitious pleasures. They form enormous groups based on emanations from the earth's surface, where millions of men and women nourish their basest needs. They sustain their temporary collective life by absorbing energies from the homes of incarnate brothers and sisters, like a large community of criminals living at the expense of a generous herd of cattle. However, we must remember that humans exploit cattle, which are unconscious and incapable of being judged for any wrongdoings, whereas in the human sphere the picture is different. Rational creatures cannot shirk their responsibilities. If persecutors that are invisible to earthly eyes form groups for the systematic worship of rebelliousness and selfishness, incarnate humans – masters of valuable patrimonies of sanctifying knowledge – ensure their disgraceful work by continually running from their divine duties as God's helpers in the area of service where they find themselves, feeding a ruinous alliance. Thus, sharing the results of destructive indifference or condemnable action, they both reciprocally torment and agitate each other like wild animals that devour one another in the jungle of life. They mutually obsess one another whether on or off the instructive pathways of the flesh. Consequently, they spend centuries yoked to one another, bound to lamentable illusions and evil purposes, causing themselves extreme disturbances, since the inheritance of heaven is completely unreachable for all those who scorn the divine seeds they carry within them. There are millions of human souls that have not yet left the surface of the planet, not even after more than ten thousand years. They die in the dense body and are reborn in it, just like trees that sprout over and over again because they are deeply rooted in the ground. Individually and collectively, they repeat multi-millennial lessons without discovering the heavenly gifts of which they are the heirs. They deliberately abandon their inner sanctuary on the shifting sand of inconsequential self-worship, from time to time fighting ruinous wars that reach both planes in a wrongly directed impulse of liberation through abominable crises of fury and suffering. Consequently, they destroy what they have laboriously built and they modify the processes of outward life from one civilization to the next."

Perceiving the close attention with which we were following what he was saying, the Instructor continued after a brief pause:

"However, in the ebb and flow of many ages, the children of the planet who were attentive to the divine determinations, and who remained free of their former slavery to moral poverty, return to the dark environment of the captivity they abandoned, in order to help their ignorant and wayward brothers and sisters in a sublime endeavor of compassion. They form the vanguards of Christ at the most diverse points of the globe, and under his guidance, millions of them work in love and selflessness, proceeding, albeit with extreme difficulty, confronting the incendiary and exterminating offensive with the blessings of the Heavenly Light."

The exposition could not have been clearer. But Eloi remarked, disconcerted:

"Who on earth – our old domicile – could ever imagine that infinite life could thus continue so strange and dreadful?"

"Indeed," agreed our guide. "Orthodoxy, however, is usually the corpse of revelation. Thousands of years of theological arguments have clouded the human mind regarding the divine realities. Even so, the individual will continue in the task of self-discovery. In the everyday struggle, the power of the mind is restricted to the narrow circle of the selfish personality, like the mollusk chained to the shell. We know that such power – the eternal patrimony with which we either sublimate or degrade ourselves – emits creative rays to the passive matter surrounding us; hence, the direction they take depends on us. If millions of luminous rays form one blazing star, it is only natural that millions of tiny rays of desperation will form a perfect hell. As heirs of the Creative Power, we generate energies wherever we may be. Isn't that perfectly intelligible? That is why the Lord ordered his heavenly advice to be put in the Divine Book: 'I stand at the door and knock.' If anyone opens the living door of the soul, there will be a truly redemptive colloquy between the Master and the Disciple. The heart is a tabernacle and the sublimation of the powers that comprise it is the only pathway of access to the higher realms."

The devoted guide gave us to understand that he had finished. He smiled benevolently and asked:

"Which of us would be so foolish as to try to fly away in a balloon that is still tied down? The human mind, tied firmly to the strongest earthly interests, offers no other symbol."

We fell silent, as our thirst for explanations had been quenched. In just a few minutes, we had gathered enough invaluable study material for a long time to come.

We walked on in silence, ecstatic before the majestic beauty of the marvelous, star-filled night.

A gentle breeze whispered wordless songs in the light foliage, and groups of friends, who passed by us from time to time, displayed the same look of happiness that was flooding the flowery grove.

Thus, bathed in unforgettable emotion, we walked toward the sanctuary where we would receive instructions for our next task, filled with trust and joy like jubilant workers walking contentedly toward the struggle, as if they were happily headed for a festival of light.

3
An Accord

Under the lyrical beams of the moon, the starry dome spread vibrations of inexpressible beauty all around us, sowing hope, joy and comfort.

Having been informed about the objectives that would lead us down to the earth's surface, part of which involved a large purgatorial colony, I made use of the pleasant time to take advantage of being with Gubio by attempting to elicit a few remarks, which were always clothed in invaluable teachings.

"I'm really amazed," I ventured respectfully, "that there are veritable expeditions in our realm for attending to a simple case of obsession."

"Incarnate men and women," began my guide with a certain vagueness in his eye, as if gazing on fleeting images of the past, "can't even imagine the extent of the concern they awaken in our circles of action. We are souls magnetized to one another in the forge of blessed experiences. In the evolutionary and redemptive novel of humankind, every spirit has a special chapter.

Tender or harsh ties of love or hate, empathy or repulsion, bind us all together. Embodied souls are kept in a temporary sleep regarding their former lives. They are immersed in the Styx[2] of the ancients, whose waters offer them, for a time, invaluable security to return to the opportunities of spiritual growth. Even so, while they are immersed in beneficent forgetfulness, we, on our part, wait in blessed wakefulness. The perils that threaten our loved ones of now or of ages that time has consumed do not allow us to remain passive. Human beings are not alone on the narrow path of their wholesome trials. The responsibility for perfecting the world falls to all of us."

After being informed about the young woman we were about to help, I asked respectfully:

"Is the sick woman we are to assist connected to your past as a spirit?"

"Yes, she is," Gubio confirmed humbly, "but I was not assigned to Margarida's case just because she was my daughter in bygone ages. In each case of assistance, one must consider the many parties involved. Due to the enigma of obsession that we're hoping to resolve, we will have to look for all the individualities that make up the picture. In every matter of assistance, large numbers of persecutors and persecuted are entwined with each other. Each spirit is an important link in the extensive region of the human chain. The more we grow in knowledge and aptitudes, love and authority, the larger the ambit of our connections within the overall circle. There are souls who are watched over with concern by millions of others. As long as the activities of life are being carried out harmoniously under the auspices of the Good, there are no problems, but when trouble arises, it isn't easy to undo the

---

2 A river that separates the world of the living from the world of the dead in Greek mythology. (www.pantheon.org.) – Tr.

obstacles, because in such circumstances we have to proceed with complete impartiality, giving each one what he or she deserves. On tormenting days, especially, incarnates usually see only 'their side of things,' but, above ordinary justice per se, higher courts are in session … Consequently, every case of spiritual disharmony on the earth creates a large network of servants here, who, based on the love that Jesus exemplified, treat them without personal inclinations. On such occasions, we get ready to satisfy all the imperatives of the rescue work that the task imposes on us or provides us amid the activities that are connected with them."

At this point in the instructive conversation, we reached a graceful temple.

In that warm retreat dedicated to the materialization of sublime spirits, the soft light of the night was as calming as it was beautiful.

The constant vibrations of many centuries of prayer had created an enchanting atmosphere around the imposing structure.

A heavenly melody wafted about and the delicate flowers in the atrium seemed to respond to the crystalline sounds, almost imperceptibly changing in brilliance and color.

I bore a heavy heart, as if the happiness of the last few hours, in which I had heard such comforting yet grave thoughts regarding the expanse of the world and life, had made me aware of my personal insignificance before the divine grandeur, and peaceful tears flooded my face.

The Instructor led us into the garden that surrounded the delightful sanctuary.

A few brothers and sisters came to welcome us.

One of them, Instructor Gama, who was in charge of the temple's services, embraced us and said kindly:

"You're right on time. Those who are going to offer their sublimated fluids are ready and the other commission is here too."

We went right in.

I was told that there was another group there that included two sisters who had come to receive work instructions for lower spheres.

A soft, bluish light bathed the large room decorated with snow-white flowers that looked like lilies.

There wasn't time for preliminary conversation.

Following brief and cordial greetings, the prayer group was arranged.

Not far away, twenty materialization mediums on our plane were ready to provide radiant energy.

In the next room, a moving melody began playing, silvery and light, putting us in the mood for lofty meditation.

Right after the lovely and spontaneous prayer by the head of the institution, the platform was surrounded by light. A shiny, milky white cloud formed, and little by little, the living, reverent figure of a venerable woman emerged from it. Her kindly gaze displayed an unspeakable serenity and she had the bearing of an ancient madonna. She greeted us with a gesture of blessing, as if sending us rays from the emerald light that formed an areola around her head.

The two women who comprised part of the service commission aside from ours approached her with discreet tears and kneeled before her.

"Mother, dear," cried one of them with such inflection in her voice that it pierced our innermost fibers, "enable me speak to you! Our longing for you is like a fire consuming our hearts. Help me! Don't let me waste this precious, divine minute!"

In spite of her tears of emotion, she continued:

"Bless us for our great journey! ... We've been waiting so long for this brief time with you ... Forgive us, dear mother, for having insisted so on seeing you ... but without your loving protection, how will we overcome the maelstrom of the abyss?"

Wishing, perhaps, to justify herself in her mother's eyes, she added in tears:

"In addition to our usual tasks in the area of service where your goodness has placed us, we have followed your loving suggestions and have been watching over Dad in the darkness for the past six years; but we have been unsuccessful ... He avoids our renewing influence and he loves the company of entities who vampirize others wherever they go. He can't even perceive our loving care, except as vague thoughts, which he easily dismisses, and if we increase our efforts to save him, he reacts like a madman. He waves his hands all about in rage, he yells blasphemies, and he begs for help from his mean companions, whose dark radiations entwine him, thereby repelling our suggestions and presence. He prefers the company of ignorant and wretched spirits, and he detests our tenderness."

A more intense emotional crisis kept her from going on.

The noble lady came down from the platform, lifted her two daughters to their feet, and tearlessly yet sadly gathering them into her arms, she exclaimed with consolation in her voice:

"My dear girls, the sun has to fight against the darkness every day. We have to fight unceasingly against evil until we are victorious. Do not think you are all alone in this dolorous conflict. Let us continue to try to forgive your father, and let us work together to restore him to the firm ground of the light. If Christ has labored for us from the beginning of time without our being able to grasp the greatness of his selflessness, what can we say about our obligations of help and tolerance for one another? Claudio will always be the creditor of our respect and gratitude despite the dreadful, secret crime that keeps him bound to the depths ... He poisoned a family member to get the material wealth he needed to offer us instruction and comfort in the physical realm. Due to his extreme devotion to the three of us, he didn't waiver before the temptation that demanded his infernal commitment. Because of his restless love, he wasn't able to wait for the blessing of time and he committed the unspeakable crime to place us in an oasis of deceitful superiority ... So that he could assure himself that we were well-off, he lived for forty years in remorse and suffering, psychically attuned to malevolent and vengeful spirits in the darkness. But in reality, because of his afflictions, we were able to live a blessed lifetime of progress and comfort in a happy and abundant home without our knowing that a dark act of murder and violence lived on our spiritual foundations!"

At this point, the materialized spirit wept emotionally.

With the three of them embraced in an emotional and wordless scene, the mother found the strength to go on:

"Let us return to the regenerative and beneficent battlefield ... What good does the heavenly landscape do us without the liberation of those we love? The loving, tormented soul will refuse to enter a star in order to remain by the side of a loved one who is dueling with serpents in a swamp ... Can we enjoy the august spectacle of the resplendent realms and listen to their indescribable harmony in a distinguished situation bought at the cost of those who cry out and perish in the darkness? To forsake someone who has helped us ascend is one of the most awful forms of ingratitude. The Lord cannot bless a happy harvest that has cost anguish for those who gathered it. I am convinced that there is more greatness in the angel who descends into hell in order to save God's wayward and suffering children than in the spirit messenger who rushes in torment before the Throne of the Eternal One to praise Him while forgetting his own benefactors."

The venerable woman wiped her copious tears and continued:

"So, my daughters, let's forget about what we are today so that we may help those who, with the purpose of serving us, have slid down the sinister and tormenting cliff. Let us liquidate our secret debts with selflessness and devotion. Later, I will receive Antonio, the nephew whom Claudio poisoned, into my maternal arms, reconciling him with Claudio through mutual cordiality and respect. With joyful tenderness, I will teach him to speak the name of God and to clear away the dark clouds of rebelliousness that have obscured his inner life. In order to incline him to understanding and mercy most effectively, I have committed myself to welcome into the maternal tabernacle the six wayward creatures of the Good, whom he madly attached himself to in the lower regions as a result of his guilt. My love will reign with difficulty in a home full of souls that will not have much in common with mine, where Jesus will teach me to happily grasp the sweet lesson of silent self-sacrifice … I will often have to deal with discord and temptation; even so, we cannot believe in sudden happiness. We must use blessed cooperation to earn that peace that Claudio dreamed about for us and which he himself did not enjoy.

"However, in order for me to reincarnate, your father has to be reborn first; otherwise, I cannot begin the new phase of our redemptive process. So, let us help each other. While I try to transform Antonio to make him more loving, you two can incline your father to reconstructive hope and meditation."

The two young women wept emotionally in anguish and joy as their illumined mother readied to say goodbye, adding:

"Do not get discouraged. Time is one of the most precious gifts from the Lord and it will help us. The future will bring us back together again in the blessed refuge of earth. Thus renewed, Claudio and I will receive many children. The two of you will be among them to give comfort to our souls. My heart will be laden with a few precious stones to polish in the daily effort, and within my soul will be two flowers – you two – whose heavenly fragrance will give me the strength I need to persevere till the end. You will be my compensation amid all my weariness ... United by imperishable love, we will work, sustained by our fragmented memories of the glorious life in the spirit world that someday will welcome us, blissful and triumphant. Let us remember Jesus and carry on."

The emissary finished, and probably aware that their time together had come to an end, the girls held her to their hearts. Their mother kissed them lovingly, and after nodding cordially towards us, she returned to the platform and disappeared in a wave of evanescent mist.

We looked at each other in tears, as if we had been allowed to rest our minds in a soft melody.

The two sisters went back to their places and we heard soothing music renewing the ambience, obviously responding to our need to modify our vibrational field.

Pondering the immeasurable kindness of the Father, I recalled the ties of love that linked me to the past, and once more I saw that all the measures of the Good are planned and patiently carried out by those who have become angel-like in the virtues of heaven. Deep down, I mourned the wasted opportunities of another time when the true understanding of life had not gladdened my spirit.

I had not yet come back to myself from that wholesome digression, when another sheet of a white substance crowned with golden tones became visible above us. Soon, dressed in light, another messenger appeared on the platform.

A gentle, sanctifying magnetism radiated from her eyes.

She was wearing a fine, radiant-blue peplos garment, and she descended, erect and dignified, gazing at us gently, looking for someone in particular.

The Instructor stood up reverently and walked toward her like a submissive disciple.

Without affectation, she spoke sentences of peace in a tone of infinite tenderness:

"Brother Gubio, I thank you for your generous cooperation. I think it is now time for me to accept your fraternal help in order to liberate my poor Gregorio. I have been waiting centuries for his renewal and penitence. Endowed with immense resources of power in a distant past, he committed heinous crimes of intelligence. As part of a dangerous organization of moral reprobates, he specialized in oppressing ignorant and wretched souls after death. Because of the hardness of his heart, he won the trust of cruel spirits as he presently performs the detestable function of a high priest of dark mysteries. He heads a condemnable phalanx of hundreds of other wretched spirits mired in evil, and they obey him with deplorable blindness and nearly-complete faithfulness. He has increased the liabilities of the clamorous debts he brought with him from his earthly madness, and he has been an unfortunate instrument in the hands of powerful and thankless enemies of the Good … Even so, for the last fifty years I've managed to approach him mentally. He was recalcitrant and hard at first, but he is now somewhat bored, which is a blessing in hearts that are unfaithful to the Lord. His mind is showing rudimentary signs of the transformation he needs. He still does not weep under the iron glove of blessed repentance and seems far from saving remorse; nonetheless, he doubts the victory of evil and harbors questions in his base mind. He is not as harsh as he used to be while commanding the unfortunate spirits that follow his orders, and I can see the collapse of his resistance not too far ahead."

I noticed that the venerable woman was shedding discreet tears that slid down her face like seeds of light.

She paused for a few moments, controlled by dolorous memories, and then continued:

"Brother Gubio, forgive my tears; they mean neither bitterness nor discouragement … According to ordinary human judgment, my son is a monster, perhaps … but to me, he is the exquisite jewel of my longing heart. I think of him as the most beautiful pearl in a sea of slime and I quake with joy when I think of seeing him again. My words are not inspired with sickly passion; they are inspired by the love that the Lord has ignited within us from the beginning. Before God, we are held by divine magnetism, just like the stars that attract one another in the empire of the universe. I will not find heaven unless Gregorio's sentiments also turn towards Wisdom Eternal. We nourish ourselves in the creation with the rays of everlasting life that we send to one another. How can I find perfect bliss if I receive only rays of misdirected energies from my beloved son?"

Our guide gazed at her with moist eyes and replied:

"Dearest Matilde, we are ready! Tell us what you would have us do! Whatever we may do for your joy, our efforts will be small and poor when compared with the sacrifices you have made on behalf of all of us."

With a sad smile, the respectable woman continued:

"In just a few years, I shall descend into the whirlwind of corporeal struggles in order to wait for Gregorio in a lifetime of difficult and dolorous redemption. I will instruct him according to the highest principles governing life. He will grow up under my immediate inspiration and will receive the perilous and afflictive trial of material riches. It is our plan that, in time and with gradual effort, he will welcome the legion of wicked servants that now follow and obey him, so that he might steer them as far as possible, both incarnate and discarnate ones, along the pathway of sanctification through beneficent discipline in constructive sweat. He will suffer slander and contempt. He will often be humiliated in people's eyes. He will be victorious in ephemeral things and deceitful honors. As his saving endeavor progresses, he will be tempted in every way by the colony of ignorance, perversity and moral delinquency that he is now connected with, and after heartbreaking experiences, he will know the desertion of false friends, abandonment, misery, old age and loneliness. He will cling to my care in childhood, adolescence and adulthood; even so, amid the harshest trials, I will precede him on the journey to the grave … At that time, however, which I can foretell even now, my maternal heart, although in the spirit realm, will encourage him step by step to victory … In the bitterness and delusions that will help him restructure and perfect the powers of his mind, my voice of eternal love will be registered precisely by him … But until then, Gubio, I must work much and optimistically, incessantly taking advantage of the time. I will set the cords of sublime intercession in motion; I will mobilize my friends, and I will pray to Jesus for strength and serenity. We will begin his deliverance with your selfless cooperation in the abysmal realm."

The venerable messenger paused briefly, and focusing her gaze on our Instructor, she added with a new inflection in her voice:

"You shall watch after Margarida, who used to be your beloved daughter, and to whom Gregorio still feels attracted by the dark web of the past. You shall also collaborate with my maternal devotion so that his soul may be converted from rebelliousness to humility, and from coldness to warmth. When you find him, wear the mantle of the worthy servant and speak to him in my name. Under the ice that has crystallized his sentiments lies the still-burning flame of the love that has always united us. I have been granted the permission to make myself perceive and believe that in light of your loving endeavor, you will move his hardened spirit.

"I know how difficult this incursion into the realms of pain will be for you, because only the one who knows how to love and endure can triumph over consciences perverted by evil; even so, my friend, the divine gifts descend upon us amid conditional disputes. The Lord has enriched us so that we may enrich others; he has given us something to practice the distribution of blessings that belong to him; he has helped us so that we may in turn help those most in need. The one who reaps the most is the one who has sown the most."

Before those divine eyes, now covered in tears that had not yet fallen, Gubio took advantage of the pause and reverently considered:

"My selfless Matilde, I am too small to deserve your words. Where there is joy, suffering cannot linger. You have aided me with your intercession, assisting me with Margarida's needs. A father's heart is always fortunate at being humbled for his beloved children. I am merely your debtor, and if Gregorio were to punish me in the spheres he controls, such affliction would also become joy within me. Whatever the case may be, he shall remind me of your goodness and devotion supporting my purpose to descend in order to serve. The pain that it may cause me would be blessed thorns in the roses you have offered me. In your name, I will save my daughter, whose current life in the dense body is highly important for our upcoming reincarnations … I shall work, aware of the opportunity you have given me; I shall struggle, encouraged and happy."

Showing intense joy and great hope on her face, the woman thanked him with kind words and concluded:

"When you complete the essential phase of your mission in the next few days, I will be notified by our messengers and will meet you in the 'exit areas'.[3] Then, who knows? It is probable that the personal meeting that I have longed for for so long will take place, because Gregorio will possibly come with you to a point where, hopefully, the manifestation of the light may be made possible before the darkness."

The glowing expression on the emissary's face intensified, displaying the sweet expectation in her soul, and she considered:

"The time has come … The Lord will be with us. There is a time to sow and a time to reap. Gregorio and I shall sow once again. We shall be mother and son once more!"

Addressing our Instructor in particular, she said ecstatically:

"May my tears of joy fall like dew upon your industrious spirit. I will follow your efforts and will come when the time is right. I believe in the victory of love when the time for us to meet shines. On that blessed day, Gregorio and the fellow spirits most attuned to him will be brought by us to the spheres of regeneration, and from those spheres of readjustment, I intend to reorganize elements before the promising future, dreaming at his side of the accomplishments we're responsible for."

Gubio said a few words of fraternal commitment.

We would work tirelessly.

We would be diligent in carrying out her loving orders.

The remarkable conversation ended amid prayers of gratitude to the Eternal Father.

---

3   The expression "exit areas" refers to boundaries between the lower and upper planes.
   – Spirit Auth.

When that living worship of immortal love was over, we said goodbye to the Christian family gathered there.

Outside, the night had become even more beautiful.

The moon reigned on a throne of soft blue, surrounded by twinkling stars.

Innumerable flowers greeted us with their inebriating fragrance.

I gazed at the Instructor with eyes full of questions, but Gubio patted me on the back and said:

"Still your mind and don't ask any questions for now. Tomorrow, we will head for our new endeavor. It will require much prudence and fraternal understanding. You can be sure that service will enlighten us with its living language."

4
In a Strange City

We set out the next day.

In response to our affable inquiries, the Instructor told us that we would be gone only a few days.

Besides taking care of our main endeavor, we would also attend to a few secondary assistance activities. As a specialist on missions of such nature, he said it was a task that he could handle by himself, but he had accepted our help not only because of his confidence in us but also because of the need to train new coworkers specialized in giving assistance in the dark realms.

After crossing several regions "in descent" with stopovers at various outposts and aid institutions, we entered a vast domain of darkness.

The sun's light looked different.

A grayish haze clouded the entire sky.

Volitation was impossible.

The vegetation looked sinister and afflicted. The trees were almost bare and the nearly-dry branches looked like arms lifted in supplication.

Large, foreboding birds that looked sort of like ravens were cawing like little winged monsters eyeing hidden prey.

What was most troubling, however, was not the bleak landscape – it was somewhat similar to others I had experienced – but the piercing appeals coming from the mire. Humanlike groans came in every tone.

I would have liked to have stayed to examine those sufferers more closely, but like other instructors, Gubio did not want to get held up by pointless curiosity.

Recalling the "dark forest" of Alighieri Dante's immortal poem, my mind was full of troubling questions.

Might those strange trees, with their withered but living foliage, be souls that had become silent sentinels of pain, just like Lot's wife, who had symbolically been turned into a pillar of salt? And those odd ravens, whose eyes shone unpleasantly in the darkness? Might they be discarnate humans being severely punished in that form? Who were those that were weeping in those vast valleys of mire? Creatures that had lived on the earth as we knew them, or goblins unknown to us?

From time to time, hostile groups of deranged spirit entities passed in front of us, indifferent and incapable of noticing our presence. They were speaking loudly in broken but intelligible Portuguese, their laughter betraying deplorable conditions of ignorance. They were dressed in sinister attire and carried implements for fighting and wounding.

We continued to descend, but the atmosphere grew suffocating. We managed to rest somehow, overcome with fatigue. After a few moments, Gubio explained:

"Like a diving suit made of absorbent material, our perispiritual bodies shouldn't react to the low vibrations of this plane if we focus our will. We are like individuals who would demonstrate their love by immersing themselves in a huge lake of slime to aid those who have adapted to it; they would get covered with the substances of the lake, patiently and courageously suffering its depressing influence. We have crossed important vibrational boundaries and we have to adjust our outer form to our surroundings so that we may be truly useful to those we plan to assist. After we complete the temporary transformation, we can then be seen by the inhabitants of this desolate place. From now on, prayer must be our only thread of communication with the Higher Realms until I can discern the best time for us to put our luminescent outer form back on. We may not be in infernal caves, but we have reached the great empire of perverse and backward intelligences who dwell close to the planet's surface, where incarnates suffer their ongoing influence. The time has come for us to make a small testimony. A large capacity for selflessness is crucial so that we may achieve our purposes. We could fail for lack of patience or want of sacrifice. For most of the backward brothers and sisters whom we meet, we will be no more than discarnates unaware of our own destinies."

We began inhaling the thick substances wafting around us, as if the air were composed of viscous fluids.

Eloi gasped, and despite my feeling of asphyxiating oppression, I tried to copy the approach of our Instructor, who, silent and extremely pale, was adjusting to the metamorphosis.

I was disoriented and noticed that our intentional integration with the elements of that lower plane was disfiguring us enormously. Little by little, we felt heavier. I felt like I had suddenly reconnected to my physical body because, although I was still in control of my own individuality, I found myself covered in dense matter, as if I had unexpectedly been forced to wear heavy armor.

After several minutes our guide urged us:

"Let's go! We are going to be nameless helpers for a while. We mustn't reveal who we are for now."

"But isn't that being deceitful?" asked Eloi, feeling better.

Gubio looked at us benevolently and explained:

"Don't you remember that Gospel passage that says not to let your left hand know what you right hand is doing? This is one such time. The Lord is not being deceitful when he gives us invisible resources of salvation without our being able to see him. In this dreary community, there are countless fellow spirits of the Good working under the same conditions. If we were to raise a provoking banner on this battleground, where ninety-five percent of the intelligences are devoted to evil and disharmony, our plans would be dashed right then and there. Hundreds of thousands of spirits here are suffering the bitter shock of having returned to reality, and they are being watched by cruel tribes of selfish, envious, and brutal spirits. To a more or less developed sensitivity, the suffering here is immeasurable."

"Is there an established government in such a strange and sinister realm?" I asked.

"Why wouldn't there be?" answered Gubio kindly. "As in the corporeal sphere, the Higher Powers have endowed this domain with a form of leadership for the time being. This great emporium of regenerative suffering is led by a satrap of unbelievable ruthlessness, who has given himself the pompous title 'Great Judge.' He is assisted by political and religious advisors who are as cold and perverse as he is. A huge aristocracy of implacable spirits controls thousands of idle, morally delinquent, sickly minds."

"Why does God allow such an atrocity?"

This time it was my co-worker who was doing the asking, once more half-frightened in light of the commitments before us.

Unperturbed, Gubio replied:

"For the same instructive reasons that God does not exterminate a human nation, when, insane with a thirst for domination, it unleashes cruel and destructive war; instead, he hands it over to the expiation of its crimes and to the misfortune it has brought upon itself, so that it can learn to become part of the eternal order that presides over universal life. Over the course of many centuries, the matter used by those intelligences is worked and restructured, just like in the earthly circles; but if the Lord visits humankind by means of sanctified individuals, he also corrects spirits by means of hardened or beastly ones."

"So, does that mean that evil spirits, demons…" I began to ask, hesitantly.

"… are we, ourselves," the Instructor patiently completed, "when we impenitently go astray of the Law. We, ourselves, used to roam these dark and troubling realms. However, the biological jolts of your more or less recent rebirth and discarnation do not allow you or Eloi to remember your pasts completely. But for me, the situation's different. The length of my time in the life of freedom has enabled me to remember things in more detail, and I know in advance the lessons that seem new to you. Many of our fellow spirits who have reached higher realms no longer see these surroundings as a reason for anything except fatigue, repugnance and dread; and yet, we must realize that this bog is actually an area of nature that requires the assistance of strong and benevolent workers."

We could hear weird music playing in the distance, and Gubio told us to be prudent and humble to ensure the success of our task.

We got up and started out again.

Our steps were slow and our progress difficult.

In a low voice our guide reiterated his recommendation:

"During any time of inner duress, we mustn't forget to pray. From this point on, prayer will be our only means for mobilizing the higher mental reserves we will need for our psychic replenishment. Any rashness could drag us down into primitive-like states and put us on a lower level much like that of the unfortunate spirits we mean to help. We must be composed and firm, gentle and bold, with our souls focused on Christ. We must remember that we have accepted this job not to judge but to educate and serve."

We pressed on as best we could.

A short time later, we entered a vast agglomeration of narrow streets lined with sordid and unkempt dwellings.

Loathsome faces eyed us furtively at first, but as we continued on our way, we were scrutinized by hostile and dreadful-looking passersby.

A few miles of public streets filled with heartrending scenes unrolled before us.

Hundreds of emotionally imbalanced entities, along with disfigured ones with all sorts of deformities, made up the horrifying picture.

Impressed by that multitude of deformed creatures, all gathered there in collective experience, I discreetly asked the Instructor a few questions.

Why such a large community of sufferers? What had they done to warrant such flagrant deformities? Always patient, Gubio did not hesitate to reply:

"After death, millions of individuals run into dangerous enemies due to fear and self-shame. In the sphere of our actions, words and thoughts, nothing is lost, Andre. The record of our lives works in two distinct phases: outside of us through the effects of our actions regarding our neighbors, situations and affairs as individuals, and within the archives of our conscience, which mathematically records all the results of our good or bad deeds. The spirit acts amid its own creations. Dark imperfections and praiseworthy qualities both envelop it wherever it may be. People on the earth, on which we journey, hear arguments alluding to heaven and hell, and they vaguely believe in the spirit life that awaits them after death. Sooner than they might think, they lose their physical body and realize they can no longer hide behind its mask like a turtle in its shell. They are seen for what they really are, and they dread the children of the light, whose gifts of penetration lay bare their blemishes right away. To the mind, the perispirit, due to its rarified composition, is a very delicate capsule that is susceptible to reflecting either its glory or corruption. Consequently, in rebelliousness against the duties that everyone is responsible for in the work of sublimation, fallen souls join forces in communities like this one, where, as much as possible, they exteriorize the lamentable inclinations peculiar to them, despite being stung by the needle of powerful and cruel intelligences."

"But aren't there any means of helping such communities?"

"The same law of self-effort applies here as well. They do not lack sanctifying appeals from On High; however, in the absence of an inner adhesion to the ideal of spiritual growth, any real initiative is impracticable regarding overall readjustment. Unless the spirit – the lord of reason and the eternal values that result from it – decides to mobilize its own patrimony to raise its vibrations, it would not be right to forcefully take it to higher spheres, to which it does not yet aspire. Until it resolves to undertake its own ascension, it will be used by the universal laws wherever it may be useful for the Divine Work. The worm

– while it is a worm – is compelled to work the soil; the fish – while it is a fish – cannot live out of the water."

Pleased with his argumentation, he concluded in a humorous tone:

"Thus, it is natural that humans – owners of countless theories regarding salvation – should be used in inferior activities while they linger in the convoy of inferiority. The Law is in perfect tandem with Logic."

Gubio paused, evidently constrained by the need for us not to call too much attention to ourselves.

However, touched by the misery that framed such suffering around us, I lost myself in a sea of inner questioning.

What kind of weird emporium was this? Some sort of country where subhuman types thrived? I knew that such creatures were not wearing physical bodies and that they were being held in this purgatorial realm for their own good; and yet, they were dressed in clothing of an obviously filthy material. Lombroso and Freud would find a lot of material for observation. There were countless types that would be of interest to criminology and psychoanalysis as they wandered aimlessly around in self-absorption. Countless examples of dwarf-like beings, whose nature I cannot yet define, passed by in hoards. Unpleasant looking, weird plants proliferated there, and herds of monstrous animals were roaming about aimlessly like oppressed beings that some heavy hand had turned into goblins. Alleys and dark precipices grew in number all around, heightening our astonished anguish.

After crossing a vast area, I could not let go of the questions escaping my brain.

The instructor explained discreetly:

"Hold on to your troubling questions for now. This is an enormous purgatorial colony. Those who are not undergoing dolorous regenerative penitence may be considered as subhuman intelligences. Thousands of creatures, utilized in the harshest work, are active in this infra-terrestrial place. For now, their ignorance does not confer the glory of responsibility on them. As they develop their dignified tendencies, they apply for incarnate humanity. They are between the fragmentary reasoning of apes and the simple ideas of primitive human beings. They can either become attached to incarnate personalities, or they can blindly obey the powerful spirits that control places like this one. They hold on to the naivety of the primitive and the faithfulness of the dog. The contact with certain individuals inclines them either to good or to evil, and we are responsible for the Superior Forces that govern us regarding the type of influence we exert on the infantile minds of such creatures. As for the animal-like human spirits on these sinister streets, we can see various examples of the abnormality resulting from our inner disharmony. Our mental activity marks our perispirit. We can affirm the truth of what I am saying, even while in the world. Gluttons start to take on a depressing aspect in their bodies. Alcoholics begin to live 'lying on their stomach,' bound to the soil like giant worms. Women who sell their bodies, thus forgetting the sacred purposes of life, display a sad countenance. But here, Andre, the devouring fire of the disgraceful passions reveals its victims with the most heinous cruelty."

Due to my concern regarding the issue of assistance, our guide continued:

"Individual, systematic care for the sick is impractical in a city with thousands of sick and alienated beings. A doctor from the world would come across hundreds of cases of amnesia, psychasthenia[4], and insanity due to complex neuroses, and

---

4 A neurotic disorder marked by phobias, obsessions, compulsions, or excessive anxiety. No longer in technical use. (The American Heritage® Stedman's Medical Dictionary, 2002). – Tr.

would reach the conclusion that every pathogeny is rooted in causes of a mental order. Time, along with heavenly mercy, can only heal in these places through the work of ambassadors of selflessness, who, inspired by goodwill, intercede for repentant spirits willing to obey the imperatives of the Law."

A number of repulsive pedestrians brushed up against us but Gubio thought it wise not to say anything.

I noticed a few service organizations that, in the physical sphere, would seem rather simple and childish due to the idleness that was their dominant trait. And because I did not see any children, except possibly those of the dwarf-like beings – whose adults I could not distinguish from the children – I risked another whispered question.

Gubio responded:

"For the people of earth per se, this plane is almost like hell. If human compassion keeps children separated from known criminals, what can be said of the love with which heavenly compassion watches over children?"

"But why such widespread idleness on this plane," I asked further.

"Almost all the human souls in these furnaces suck the energy out of incarnates and vampirize their lives like insatiable lampreys in the ocean of earth's oxygen. They long to return to the physical body, since they haven't yet improved their minds enough to go higher, and they pursue the emotions of the corporeal realm with the madness of people dying of thirst in the desert. Like overdue fetuses absorbing their mothers' energies, they consume large amounts of energy from the incarnates that nurture them, unaware of a superior knowledge. Hence the desperation with which they defend the powers of inertia and the aversion with which they regard any spiritual progress or any human advancement up the mountain of sanctification. At heart, these spirits still live in the sphere of ordinary humans, and thus they passionately hold on to the system of psychic theft that feeds them."

We came to an area of uneven ground, which the Instructor led us across.

Then, we ascended a steep road, until a small plateau opened before our fearful eyes. The scenery changed.

Strange, impressive palaces appeared, illuminated by some sort of ember-like light similar to the glow of incandescent steel.

Well-tended, crowded squares showed ostentatious carts pulled by slaves and animals.

The sight reminded us of the great cities of the Orient two hundred years ago.

Litters and carriages were bearing individuals dressed in predominantly-red garments, accentuating the hardness of the faces that emerged from them.

An impressive edifice, with all the characteristics of a temple, stood out across from a fortress. Our guide confirmed my impressions, stating that the place was used for worship rituals.

While we were admiring the opulent palace, a shocking contrast to the vast realm of misery we had just crossed, someone approached and rudely asked:

"What are you doing here?"

It was a tall man with a hooked nose and feline eyes, with all the mannerisms of a disrespectful policeman asking for identification.

"We are looking for Gregorio, the priest; we were recommended to him," Gubio explained humbly.

The man told us to follow him and he took us to an ugly-looking mansion.

"He lives here!" he said dryly. He introduced us to an older man wearing a complex-looking robe and left.

Gregorio did not welcome us kindly. He glared at Gubio with the suspicious eyes of a startled beast and asked:

"Did you arrive from the earth very long ago?"

"Yes," replied our Instructor, "and we need your help."

"Have you been examined yet?"

"No."

"Who sent you?" asked the priest.

"A certain messenger named Matilde."

Our host trembled, but remarked implacably:

"Never heard of her. Even so, you may come in. I have to attend to the mysteries and I can't help you right now. But tomorrow night you will be taken to the selection department before being admitted to my service."

He had nothing else to say.

We were handed over to an unpleasant-looking servant who led us down into a dark basement. I must confess that I accompanied Gubio and Eloi with a soul troubled with absorbing and indefinable dread.

5
A Selective Procedure

That night, after several hours of meditating and praying in a dark room, without anyone saying a word, we were taken to a large, curious-looking building.

The strange palace was shaped like a huge hexagon with brownish spires rising into the air. There were several rooms dedicated to odd services. Illuminated both inside and out by large torches, the place had the unpleasant aspect of a building on fire.

In the custody of four of Gregorio's guards, who told us that we would have to be examined before having any direct contact with the priest, we entered a large hall containing a few dozen deplorable-looking entities.

Old and young, men and women were wandering around in relative silence.

Some were moaning and weeping.

I could see that nearly all of them were sickly. Several were obviously mentally ill.

Impressed, I studied their sickly aspect.

Their perispirits were as opaque as a physical body. The stigmas of old age, disease and disenchantment, which dog the human experience, were completely victorious.

Fear controlled the most desperate because the silence was stifling, although anxiety was plainly visible on every face.

A few servants wearing characteristic garb were separating the discarnates into several groups as they entered in order to be selected and tried.

The Instructor explained discreetly:

"The merciless judges who live here perform this ceremony every week. The selection process is based on the radiations emitted by each subject. Certain colors characterize the auras of ignorant, perverse and imbalanced spirits, and the guards in charge of doing the selecting are technicians that identify various ills indicated by such colors. This selection process makes the judges' work easier and thus more thorough."

Gregorio's men gave us some room but they kept an eye on us from the crowded galleries.

Thankfully, the personnel doing the selecting did not split the three of us up but put us in with the rest of the victims.

After listening to Gubio's explanation, I asked:

"Were all these spirits constrained to come here just like us? Are there really satanic spirits, like the ones in religious paintings, fighting for souls on the deathbed?"

"Yes, Andre, each mind lives amongst the company it has chosen. The same principle applies for those who live within the dense body or outside of it. It is important to realize, however, that most of the souls in this place are here due to the forces of attraction. They were incapable of perceiving the presence of the spirit benefactors who work among incarnates in endeavors of self-denial and benevolence, and due to their low vibrational level resulting from repeated wrongs, impenitent idleness, or willful crystallization in error, they found nothing but darkness all around them. Alone and confused, they went looking for discarnates with whom they had an affinity and they naturally met in this immense hive carrying the whole load of the destructive passions that characterized their journey. When such souls get here, however, they must endure the watchfulness of the powerful and hardened intelligences who rule like dictators in these regions, where the bitter fruits of evil and indifference fill the storehouse of unprepared and malicious hearts."

"Ah!" I exclaimed under my breath, "Why does the Lord confer the attributes of judges on such despotic spirits? Why is justice in this strange city in the hands of diabolical leaders?"

Gubio gave me a meaningful look and added:

"Who would dare appoint an angel of love to perform the role of tormenter? Also, just like in the corporeal realm, every position after death is occupied by those who want it and look for it."

I looked around and was overcome with compassion. In that community of victims, herded together like rare animals for a feast, humility and affliction held sway; but among the sentinels, the poison of irony was overflowing.

Swear words were disrespectfully shouted at random.

One irreverent crowd was in front of a large, unmanned platform and right under the side galleries packed with onlookers.

After a few unpleasant and oppressive minutes, a loud voice was heard:

"The judges! The judges! Make way! Make way for the priests of justice!"

Curious, I tried to look outside. I saw officials dressed exactly like lictors of ancient Rome, carrying the symbolic axe *(fasces5)* on their shoulders and flanked by servants holding big torches to light the way. They entered the courtroom in rhythmic steps, and after them came seven oddly-dressed judges sitting on seven sedan-chairs carried by various dignitaries.

What kind of religious ceremony was this? Those chairs were identical to the *sedia gestatoria6* used in Papal ceremonies.

The lictors entered the court, put their symbolic instruments aside and stood in front of the large platform, over which an alarming torch blazed.

The judges descended pompously from their thrones and took their seats in a kind of alcove, inspiring silence and fear, because the mindless throng suddenly grew quiet.

A number of drums rolled, as if we were at a military parade, and semi-wild music accompanied their rhythm, grating on our nerves.

When the noise ended, one of the judges stood up and addressed the crowd somewhat in these terms:

"Neither tears nor lamentations.

"Neither condemnation nor gratuitous acquittal.

"This court neither punishes nor rewards.

"Death is the road to justice.

"Any recourse to compassion is useless among criminals.

"We do not mete out suffering but we are stewards of the Government of the World.

"Our job is to divide up moral delinquents so that the punishments wrought by their own wills may be duly applied at the right place and time.

---

5   The word *fasces* means "bundle" and refers to the fact that it is a bundle of rods, which surrounded an ax in the middle. www.livius.org/fa-fn/fasces/fasces. - Tr.

6   The portable throne on which the Pope used to be carried on certain solemn occasions. - Oxford Dictionary of the Christian Church. – Tr.

"Those who opened their mouths to vilify and hurt must be ready to receive the dreadful energies they unleashed through their poisonous words.

"Those who relished slander will have to endure the unfortunate beings to whom they lent their ears.

"Those who misused their eyesight on hatred and disorder will discover new energies to contemplate the results of the imbalance they willingly took part in.

"Those who used their hands to sow malice, dissention, envy, jealousy and deliberate trouble must be prepared to reap thorns.

"Those who focused their senses on abusing their sacred faculties will feel maddening needs from now on, because debasing passions, harbored by the soul in the physical body, will explode here. For a long time, the flood-gate has kept microbes and monsters away from the peaceful course of the waters; even so, a time comes when the storm or decadence overpowers the stone dam, and set free, the repellent forms spread and grow all along the current.

"Followers of vice and crime, tremble!

"You have condemned yourselves. You have kept your minds prisoner to the lowest forces of life, like the amphibians, which, over the course of the centuries, have grown accustomed to being stuck in the slime of the swamp!"

The speaker paused and I examined his audience.

Everyone's eyes were wide open with fear.

The judge did not show a trace of mercy. He was only interested in creating a negative atmosphere instead of any sort of moral edification, establishing downright fear in his listeners.

As the pause continued, I shot a look of silent questioning at our guide, who replied in a whisper:

"The judge is fully aware of the magnetic laws of the lower spheres, and is trying to destructively hypnotize his victims, despite using the blunt truth, as we've seen."

"It does no good to complain about the way this colony is run," the booming voice continued, "because none can escape the consequences of their own deeds, just as the fruit cannot run from the properties of the tree that produced it.

"May all who disrespect our decisions be cursed by the World Government, for our decisions are based on each person's own mental files."

Intuitively perceiving his audience's mental complaints, he roared terrifyingly:

"Who accuses us of being cruel? Is not a prison warden a benefactor of the human collective spirit? And who are you, if not just human rubbish. Did you not come here led by the idols you worshipped?"

At that remark, many were overcome with convulsive weeping.

Tormented cries begging for mercy were heard. Several fell to their knees.

Overwhelming grief had taken over.

Gubio placed his right hand on his chest as if holding his heart. For my part, as I watched that large group of rebellious, humiliated, prideful and defeated spirits bitterly regretting wasted opportunities, I recalled my own former ways of illusion and – why not admit it? – I too kneeled in repentance, silently begging for mercy.

Enraged, the judge bellowed angrily:

"Forgiveness? Did you ever sincerely forgive your companions in life? Show me just one righteous judge that offers mercy with impunity.

And using his hands to focus all his magnetic power on a poor woman who was staring at him in dismay, he commanded her in a somber voice:

"Come here! Come here!"

Looking hypnotized, the poor wretch obeyed the order, emerged from the crowd and placed herself under the forceful rays of his attention.

"Confess! Confess!" ordered the ruthless judge, aware of the fragile and passive being he was addressing.

The poor woman smote her breast, as if reciting the Confiteor[7], and cried out in sorrow:

"Forgive me! Forgive me, O my God!"

As if under the power of some mysterious drug that made her expose her innermost self to all of us, she spoke in a loud, halting voice:

"I killed four innocent little children ... and I hired the murder of my unbearable husband ... But my crime is a living monster. It persecuted me while I was in the physical body ... I tried to run from it by every means possible, but it was useless ... and the more I tried to drown my wretchedness in 'drinking for pleasure,' the more I wallowed ... in the mire of my own self."

Suddenly, appearing to experience the interference of loathsome memories, she clamored:

"I want wine! Wine! Pleasure!"

In a forceful demonstration of power, the judge stated triumphantly:

"How can prayers and tears liberate such a human beast?"

Then, fixing the radiations from his fearsome look on her, he proclaimed peremptorily:

"She has condemned herself! She is nothing but a she-wolf, a wolf, a wolf..."

---

7   The Confiteor (so called from the first word, *confiteor*, I confess) is a general confession of sins; it is used in the Roman Rite at the beginning of Mass and on various other occasions as a preparation for the reception of some grace. Fortescue, Adrian. "Confiteor." The Catholic Encyclopedia. Vol. 4. New York: Robert Appleton Company, 1908. 12 Jun. 2010 <http://www.newadvent.org/cathen/04222a.htm>. – Tr.

As he repeated those words, as if trying to persuade her to feel like an animal, I saw the deeply impressionable woman's face begin to change. Her mouth twisted, the neck curved spontaneously forward, and her eyes changed in their sockets. Her face took on a wolf-like look.

In that display of power, I was obviously witnessing the effect of hypnotism on her perispiritual body.

Gubio explained in a whisper:

"Remorse is, of course, a blessing that leads us to make amends, but it is also a breach through which one's creditor demands payment. Hardness congeals our sensibility for a certain amount of time; and yet, a time always comes when remorse opens our mental life to the jolts of our own emissions coming back to us."

In a barely audible voice, he added:

"We are witnessing the genesis of the phenomenon of lycanthropy, which is still impenetrable to the research of incarnate doctors. Do you remember Nebuchadnezzar, the powerful king referred to in the Bible? The Holy Book tells us that, for seven years, he lived as if he were an animal. Hypnotism is as old as the world itself and has been used by good and bad individuals alike. It is based primarily on the pliable elements of the perispirit."

Noticing that the unfortunate woman still had the strange facial features, I asked:

"Will that poor sister keep such a degrading appearance from now on?"

After a long pause, the Instructor replied sadly:

"She would not have to endure such humiliation if she didn't deserve it. Moreover, even though she has conformed to the forceful energies of the cruel judge, into whose hands she has fallen, she can still make an inner effort to renew her mental life for the supreme good and attune herself to the influence of benefactors who are never scarce on the redemptive path. In cases like this, Andre, everything is a matter of attunement. Our life will develop where we put our thoughts."

Our guide could not continue.

Lamentations grew louder all around us.

There was no end to the interjections of dread and grief.

The judge ordered silence and scolded the wailers for their attitude. Then, he announced that the Selector Spirits would materialize shortly and that those who were interested could ask of them any explanations they wanted. At the same time, he raised his hands reverently, and showing that he was in control of the strange gathering, he uttered a loud invocation, indicating his status as a hierophant to be respected with great solemnity.

When he had finished his speech, a large cloudy layer appeared over the platform, which had been empty until then.

Little by little, before our astonished eyes, three spirits took perfect human form. The one with the most hierarchical authority held a small crystalline instrument in his hands.

They were wearing robes of a curious, indefinable bright yellow substance, and had dull, reddish auras. The aureole was more prominently vivid around the head and was sending out disturbing radiations that looked like the glow from red-hot iron.

His two acolytes took documents from a nearby coffer and followed him as he descended toward us in silence.

The turbulent crowd was suddenly quiet.

I did not yet know what secret organization those spirits came from; however, I did notice that the head of the trio wore a deeply melancholic look on his face.

He lifted the crystalline instrument in front of the first group, composed of fourteen men and women of various types. He made some remarks that I could not follow, and then said something to his companions, who immediately wrote something down. But before he moved on, two members of the group begged for help:

"Justice! Justice!" begged the first. "I'm being punished for something I didn't do ... I was a man of thought and learning among incarnates ... Why do I have to put up with the company of the avaricious?"

And looking at the selector in anguish, he added,

"If you judge fairly, then release me from this labyrinth."

He had not finished when the second broke in:

"Venerable judge, whoever you are! ...I am not one of the avaricious. I have been thrown in with sordid and despicable beings! I spent my life surrounded by books, not money ... Science fascinated me; studies were my favorite task ... So how can an intellectual be classified as a usurer?"

The leader of the selectors had a look of reserved pity on his calm face and explained firmly:

"You complain in vain, because unpleasant vibrations of selfishness characterize every one of you. What did you do with the educational treasure you were given? Your 'vibrational tone' shows sarcastic avarice. Those who accumulate degrees and books, theories and scientific values, without sharing them to benefit others, are unfortunate brothers and sisters of those who hoard money and equities, titles and precious objects without helping anyone. The same plate serves both of them on the scale of life."

"For God's sake!" one of the onlookers begged in tears.

"This is a house of justice in the name of the Government of the World!" the judge remarked calmly.

And impassive, although visibly embittered, he moved on to the next group.

He began scrutinizing a group of eight individuals; however, as he was communicating with his aids regarding his observations, a man with a cadaverous face shouted furiously:

"What's going on in this weird place? I'm in the midst of a bunch of confessed slanderers, whereas I performed the role of a respectable man ... I raised a large family; I never betrayed my social duties; I was respectable and dignified; despite retiring early, I fulfilled every duty that the world had given me."

With a touch of rage, he continued:

"Who is accusing me? ... Who is accusing me?"

The selector explained serenely:

"Your condemnation comes from you, yourself. You slandered your own body, creating obstacles and illnesses for it that existed only in your imagination, which was interested in avoiding beneficial and redemptive work. You assigned deplorable deficiencies and illnesses to healthy organs just so you could retire early. You succeeded. You used your friends, you subordinated criminal consciences, and you received paid rest for forty years during which you did nothing but sleep and make useless conversation. Now, it is reasonable that your vital circle is attuned to all those who have become immersed in the bog of slander."

The wretch had no will to argue. In tears, he yielded to the argument and went back to his place.

Upon reaching the third group, composed of several women, he had barely applied the odd instrument to their vibrational field when he was approached by a dreadfully disfigured woman who complained to his face.

"Why such humiliation?" she asked in copious tears. "I had a home that required a lot of work and I came here surrounded by special considerations because of my social status. So why am I stuck here with these shameful women? I am of the nobility; who are the officials who are forcing me to live with these whores?"

A fit of tears choked her voice.

With a composure that bordered on iciness, the judge stated flatly:

"This is a realm where mistakes rarely happen. Ask your own conscience. Were you really the overseer of a respectable home, as you say? Your vibrational level shows that your sanctified, female energies were abused. Your mental files contain emotional irregularities that will take a long time for you to redeem. It doesn't look like your home was your favorite place."

The woman yelled, gestured and complained, but the selector carried on.

When he reached us, he applied the instrument, which displayed tiny mirrors, and spoke to his assistants, defining our status:

"Neutral entities."

He fixed his piercing gaze on us, as if silently guessing our hidden intentions, and moved on.

Gubio explained:

"We're not being accused of anything. We will be able to do what we came to do."

"What sort of instrument was that?" asked Eloi, anticipating my curiosity.

"It's a mental wave receiver. A personalized selection would take too long. The authorities who rule this region favor group assessment, which is possible due to the colors and vibrations of the vital circle that surrounds each of us."

"Why did he say we were neutral?" I asked.

"The apparatus is not capable of determining the status of minds from our sphere. It is used for identifying imbalanced perispirits and does not reach the higher zone."

"But why does he speak in the name of the 'Government of the World'?"

The Instructor made an expressive gesture and added:

"Andre, don't forget that this is a plane of somewhat dense matter, not one of glorious sanctity. Don't forget the word 'evolution' and remember that the worst crimes of earthly civilizations have been committed in the name of the Divinity. While in the physical body, how many times did we see cruel sentences issued by ignorant minds in God's name?"

After some time, the ceremony ended with the same pompousness in which it began, and under the watchful eye of the sentinels, we returned to our starting point with unexpected meditations and profound thoughts.

6
Observations and New Discoveries

Back at Gregorio's place, we were taken from our dark cell to a room with barred windows. Everything was unpleasing to the eyes. We obviously owed the change to the encouraging result of the selection process, but actually, even here we found ourselves in a veritable dump. At any rate, it was immensely comforting to be able to gaze out at a few stars through the mist that was besieging the nighttime landscape.

The Instructor, well experienced in such expeditions, told us not to touch the metal bars because they were electrified, adding that we were still prisoners.

Nonetheless, we were able to look at the world outside and could see that the scenery was worth studying.

There was a lot of movement out on the street, where several groups of individuals were engaged in conversation not far from us.

These conversations were surprising. Nearly all of them had to do with the corporeal realm.

Minor and petty issues of private life were analyzed with obvious interest; and yet, the dominant tone was sentimental imbalance and the primary emotions were those of the physical experience.

By means of the various colors, I was able to perceive different expressions in the "vibrational auras" that clothed the individuals' personalities.

I turned to Gubio for clarification.

"You still haven't grasped the extent of the exchanges between incarnates and discarnates," he answered solicitously. "At certain hours of the night, three quarters of the population of both hemispheres are brought in contact with our realm and most of them, semi-freed from their bodies through the influence of natural sleep, are detained in low vibrational circles like this one. The painful dramas that play out in the physical realm are forged in places like this. Great crimes are conceived here, and if it were not for the active and persistent work of the protector spirits who watch over human beings in the sacrificial labor of secret charity and persevering education under Christ's supervision, even more tragic events would terrify humankind."

With my soul turned to the notions of the immense life suggested by that environment, I pondered the steady course of human civilization. Lofty thoughts cleared my mind. The Lord's goodness does not force its way into the heart. The Divine Kingdom is born within it, and like the mustard plant, it breaks free from its seed to steadily grow and thrive under the constructive impulses of the individual.

A paradise enjoyed without effort is such a presumptuous concept!

Gubio perceived my thoughts and tried to help out:

"Yes, Andre, the crown of wisdom and love is won through evolution, hard work and the individual's attunement to the purposes of the Creator. The march of civilization is slow and painful. Enormous conflicts are crucial for the spirit to develop its inner light. Incarnates live on three different planes at once. Like the tree that sets down roots in the soil, incarnates have temporary roots in the physical life; they spread out branches of sentiments and desires into the circles of lighter matter, like the plant reaching for the sky; and they are nurtured by the subtle principles of the mind, just as the tree lives on its own sap. In the tree, we have the root, the foliage and the sap – three different processes keeping it alive; and in human beings, we have the dense body of flesh, the perispiritual body made of a more rarefied matter, and the mind – all three representing the distinct expressions of life support working toward the same end. According to what we have observed, in order to sustain themselves in the evolutionary arena, incarnates need relative security biologically, nourishment for their emotions in their individual psychic lives, and a mental basis in their inner world. Life is everyone's heritage, but directing it is each one's responsibility. The fallen intelligence tumbles into the abyss, and within the lower circles in which it decides to live, it finds millions of inferior lives with whom it is used by the Heavenly Wisdom for the greater glorification of the divine work. In the economy of the Lord, nothing is lost and every resource is used in the chemistry of the Infinite Good. Right here in this city, there was, at first, a veritable realm of primitive lives. Little by little, it has become inhabited by huge communities of prideful and cruel souls. They have become entrenched here, holding to the insane purpose of fighting against Highest Goodness, yet they play a useful role with their enormous, still-sub-human groups, despite their work, which we might regard as unbearable. They use large amounts of violence; even so, over the course of the years, their intellectual influence will bring great benefits to those who are currently oppressed, and we can be certain that, despite their proud show of intelligence and power, they will remain at their posts only as long as the Divine Direction consents to it, founded on the principle that each group must have the government it deserves."

The Instructor paused at length while I focused my attention on two women who were talking close to the bars.

One of them was already discarnate and was telling her still-incarnate companion, who was partially free on the wings of sleep:

"I've noticed that you seem weaker, more submissive lately ... Are you discouraged about the commitments you made?"

Feeling a little confused, the other woman explained:

"Joao has joined a prayer circle, which has sort of been changing our lives."

The other could not believe it, and like a surprised animal, she exclaimed:

"Prayer?! Are you blind to the danger of what that means? Those who pray become submissive. You have to scorn, torment and hurt him so his rebelliousness will keep him in our sphere. If he becomes compassionate, it will ruin our plan and he will no longer be a useful instrument."

The other, however, remarked naively:

"He says he feels calmer, more confident..."

"Marina," the other interrupted angrily, "you know that we can't perform miracles and that it isn't right to accept rules and trickery from cowardly spirits, who, in the pretext of religious faith, ascribe to themselves the role of dictators of salvation. We need your husband and all the others, who, like him, live on our level. Our plan is enormous and of great importance to us! Have you forgotten how much we suffered? I myself have hard lessons to pay back."

And patting her friend's shoulder, she added:

"Don't believe in any spiritual spells. Reality is ours and we have to fully seize the opportunity. Return to your body and don't give in one inch. Run from those self-appointed apostles. They are bad for us. Take up all of Joao's time and don't let him go. Wound him slowly. He will finally get desperate and with his outbursts of disobedience displayed in our favor, we will achieve our purposes. No tolerance. Don't worry about promises of heaven or hell after death. Life is always what we make of it."

Speechless at what I had just heard, I noticed that the cunning and vengeful spirit was enveloping the other one in dark fluids, as common hypnotizers do.

I looked questioningly at our instructor, who, after having carefully watched the scene, informed us:

"There are millions of cases of this level of obsession. That poor woman is wavering in her faith and is unable to appreciate the happiness the Lord has granted her in a dignified and peaceful marriage. She will wake up early in the morning with a suspicious and smitten soul. Oscillating between 'believing' and 'not believing', she won't be able to polarize her mind in the trust with which she must face the difficulties ahead and wait for the sanctifying manifestations from On High. Due to the inner uncertainty that characterizes her attitude, she will remain attached to this ignorant and unhappy sister, who is persecuting and subjugating her in order to wreak deplorable vengeance. She will thus become an object of affliction for her husband and will endanger his incipient achievements."

"How can she break free of such an enemy?" asked Eloi.

"By maintaining a standard of superior firmness and a sufficient yearning for the Good. With such noble and ongoing effort, she would enhance her mental principles and enjoy the sublime sources of life, and instead of absorbing sickly and depressive radiations, she would begin to emit transforming and constructive ones on behalf of herself and the spirits with her. In every scene of the universe, we are one another's satellites. The strongest hold the weakest in their orbit; but we must remember that the most fragile today can become truly powerful tomorrow, according to their individual efforts. We send out and receive magnetic rays at the same time. Consequently, it is important to remember that those who are under the control of blind energies, and who yield to the blows and suggestions of the tyrannical forces emitted by the perverse intelligences who assail them, remain as receptors of psychic disorder for a long time. It is very difficult to readjust someone who doesn't want to be readjusted. Ignorance and rebelliousness are actually the breeding ground for suffocating evils."

During a spontaneous pause, I noticed, not far from us, a number of quivering, dark forms that seemed to be linked to the personalities we were studying. They looked like small egg-shaped spheres, each one slightly bigger than a human skull. They displayed different characteristics. A few were moving under their own power like giant amoebas living and breathing in that spiritual atmosphere; others, however, remained motionless, apparently inert, connected to the vital aura of individuals as they moved about.

I stared at that scene for a long time with the inquiring attitude of a lab technician looking at unknown forms.

A large number of the spirits who were parading by close to the bars were bearing such living spheres, as if the latter were attracted to the radiations of the former.

I had never seen such a phenomenon before.

In our colony, even when we were treating troubled and suffering individuals, the field of emanations was always normal. And when working alongside imbalanced souls on the planet's surface, I had never seen this particular irregularity, at least from what I had been allowed to observe.

I was troubled and turned to our instructor for help.

"Andre," he answered, circumspect, showing the seriousness of the matter, "I can understand your amazement. I saw right away that you are new to this type of work, but surely you have heard of a 'second death'."

"Yes, I have. I have accompanied several friends to the endeavor of reincarnation, when, attracted by the imperatives of evolution and redemption, they returned to the physical body. At other times, although more rarely, I received news from friends who had lost their perispiritual vehicle[8] upon entering higher realms. Those noble missionaries were distinguished by lofty titles in the higher life and I was unable to follow them closely."

Gubio smiled and remarked:

"So, you know that the perispiritual vessel is also transformable and perishable, even though it is made up of more-rarefied matter."

"Yes…" I answered hesitantly in my eagerness to learn.

"Then you have seen spirits who dissolved it as they moved on to sublime spheres, and whose greatness we are unable to fathom, for now. You have also observed brothers and sisters whose perispirits underwent reductive and disintegrating procedures in order to be reborn in earthly flesh. The former are ennobled and glorious servants who have successfully fulfilled their duties, whereas the latter are our colleagues who deserved reincarnation due to intercessory prayers. But just as what

---

8   Later, the perispirit will be the object of broader studies in Christian Spiritist schools. – Spirit Auth.

happens to those two types of spirits, ignorant, bad, wayward and criminal spirits also lose their perispiritual form after a while. Due to the density of their minds, saturated with inferior impulses, they cannot grow spiritually, and they gravitate around the absorbing passions that for many years they made the focus of their interests. A great many in such circumstances, especially participants in condemnable crimes, are attracted to their former accomplices. If followers of Jesus stay connected to Him through imponderable threads of love, inspiration and recognition, the pupils of hatred and perversity stay united under the guidance of intelligences that weave them into a web of evil. To enrich the mind with new knowledge, to perfect its faculties of expression, to purify it in the illuminative currents of the Good, and to ennoble it through the definitive incorporation of dignified principles is to develop our glorious body – as the apostle Paul expressed it – in sublimated and divine matter. That matter, Andre, is the type of vehicle we aspire to when we refer to the life that is above us. We are still held to the cellular agglutinations of the physio-perispiritual elements, just as the turtle is shackled to its shell. We immerse ourselves in the fluids of the flesh and free ourselves from them in a vicious see-saw effect through many lifetimes until we awaken our mental life to sanctifying expressions. We are like trees in the soil. Our emotional roots are immersed to various degrees within the spheres of primitive animality. Then, the scythe of death comes and cuts off our branches of earthly desires; and yet, our connections retain an extreme vitality in the lower layers and we are reborn among those same individuals whom we have associated with for a long time through shared struggles and to whom we are fettered by the communion of interests of our evolutionary line."

The explanation was lovely and new to my ears; consequently, I silenced the questions wandering about in my soul and attentively registered the Instructor's considerations as he continued:

"Physical life is a purely educational stage in the midst of eternity, and no one is called to it to partake of paradises of favor, but to the living molding of heaven in the sanctuary of the spirit, making the most of the opportunities we receive to perfect our mental qualities by growing and developing from the divine seeds we have brought with us. The incessant work for the Good, the sublimation of our motives in the transitory experience, the disciplining of our personal impulses, giving broad course to the noblest manifestations of our sentiments, and perseverance in the infinite Good – these lead to mental growth, with the acquisition of light for life everlasting. All individuals are born on the earth to enrich themselves by working for society as a whole. Sacrificing oneself is to overcome oneself, thereby earning the Greater Life. That is why Christ said that the greatest in the Kingdom of Heaven is the one who is dedicated to serving all. People can be feared and respected on earth because of the titles they have acquired by means of human convention, but if they do not progress in the realm of ideas by improving and perfecting themselves, they will have a narrow and sickly mind. In short, taking on physical matter and returning to the field of endeavor in which we find ourselves at present entails submitting ourselves to profound biological shocks meant for expanding the divine elements that will be part of our glorious form someday."

And because he saw me in the posture of a learner who wonders in silence, Gubio asserted:

"So that I may be clearer, let's take another look at the symbol of the tree. The physical vessel is the plant per se, which is limited in space and time; the perispiritual body is the fruit that consubstantiates the result of the many operations of the tree after a certain period of maturation; and the mental matter is the seed, which represents the substratum of the tree and the fruit, condensing their experiences. In order to acquire wisdom and love, individuals are reborn many, many times in the physiological field, like a seed returning to the soil. And those who deliberately make matters hard for themselves by departing from the straight path and heading for the irregular zones, where they have unwholesome experiences, will, of course, delay their progress and will waste a lot of time trying to get out of the perilous terrain they relegated themselves to. They will be connected with unhappy groups of fellow spirits who have thoughtlessly lost their way due to grave debts. Do you now understand?"

In spite of the instructor's kindness in trying to clarify the matter, I dared ask:

"Could we communicate with those living spheroids? Could they hear us? Do they have any capacity for tuning in to us?

Gubio answered kindly:

"Yes, of course. But bear in mind that, in such a situation in lower realms like this one, most of them are asleep in strange nightmares. They register our calling to them but their answers are vague. In the new form in which they are isolated, they cannot express themselves fully without the denser vehicles they lost, a fact that worsens their debt resulting from idleness or the practice of evil. In fact, you can look at them as fetal or mental 'amoebas' that can be used by perverse or rebellious spirits. The pathway of such brothers and sisters is reincarnation on the earth or in some other sector of community life, much like what happens to a seed that is placed in a dark pit for works of production, selection, and improvement. Of course, during times of transition, spirits undergoing natural evolution do not experience painful phenomena like the ones we are looking at here. The sheep that proceeds firmly along the right pathway can always count on the benefits resulting from the shepherd's guidance; however, those that stray off the pathway to indulge in adventures will not always find agreeable or constructive surprises."

My guide paused for a moment and then asked:

"So, do you see the importance of an earthly existence?"

Yes, my own experience had taught me the value of a corporeal life; but here, as I stared at those living spheroids, those sad human minds without instruments of manifestation, my respect for the material vessel grew enormously. I fully grasped the sublime meaning of Christ's words: "Walk while you still have light." The subject was fascinating and I would like to have examined it more closely, but Gubio, without betraying his characteristic politeness, suggested that I wait until the following day.

7
A Painful Sight

In the morning, a sour-looking emissary from the priest Gregorio notified us that we could enjoy some freedom until the first hours of the afternoon, when Gregorio would meet with us for a private conversation.

We left the cubicle, feeling sincerely relieved.

The night had been quite troubling, at least for me because I had not been able to rest at all. Not only had the outside noises been ongoing and disagreeable, but the atmosphere had also been heavy and suffocating. The imbalanced conversations in the environment struck and troubled me.

Gubio invited us for a little instructive walk, assuring me kindly:

"Andre, let's see if we can make use of a few minutes to study the 'ovoids'."

Eloi and I gladly went with him.

The street was packed with individuals displaying abnormalities.

Cripples of all kinds, mentally impaired spirits with various features, and men and women with tormented faces were coming and going. They were perfect examples of mental alienation. Except for a few who glared at us suspiciously and cruelly with a manifest expression of evil, most of them, in my opinion, seemed somewhere between ignorance and primitivism, between amnesia and despair. Many displayed anger at our calmness. Due to the widespread disrepair and debris, I concluded that the collective effort of maintenance lacked any sort of methodical service regarding the matter on that plane. Idle talk was the dominant trait.

The Instructor told us most assuredly that, generally speaking, lost minds struggle with fixated, implacable and obsessing ideas, and they take a long time to readjust. Debased by their own actions, they lose the notion of good taste, constructive comfort and sanctifying beauty, and they wind up in deplorable slovenliness.

In fact, the scene left much to be desired as far as order was concerned. The buildings, except for the palaces in the government square, where we could see the activities of a large number of slaves, looked completely rundown. The walls, coated with a substance that looked like slime, were not only repugnant to look at but also fetid.

Everywhere, the vegetation was scarce and withered.

Human cries – the result of suffering and unconsciousness – were frequent, provoking our sincere pity.

If the unhappy passers-by had been few enough in number, one might consider offering methodical, personal assistance; but what could one say about a whole city inhabited by obvious lunatics? In a hive of that sort, mightn't the healthy person who tried to offer help to the spirit as a whole be regarded by them as the one who was actually crazy? That was why any kind of visible charitable organization would be unworkable, except the kind of service that our Instructor was performing, that is, self-denial in sanctifying work for Christ.

Besides the prevailing disturbances, capable of starting a war of nerves in more-stable individuals on the physical plane, a suffocating fog hung in the air and we could barely make out the distant horizon.

Through a thick curtain of smoke, the origin of which I could not determine, the sun looked like a ball of clotted blood.

Eloi tried hard to inject a little humor and asked if hell might be an asylum of such vast proportions as this, to which our guide nodded and said that ordinary individuals had only a faint idea of the importance of mental creations in their lives.

Gubio explained that the mind studies, designs, determines and materializes its own desires in the matter that surrounds it, and that matter, which molds its impulses, is continuously formed by countless inferior lives undergoing the process of evolution in the scenes of the infinite universe.

We pressed on, winding through long labyrinths until we found ourselves standing in front of a large building, which, to be kind, we will call an asylum for vulnerable spirits.

If I had been incarnate, it would have been extremely hard for me to believe in a picture like the one that unfolded before our troubled eyes. No suffering after the death of the body had ever touched my heart so deeply.

The screams around us were just terrible.

We passed along a slime-covered wall, and after walking a little further, the awful scene opened up in full view. We saw a long, deep valley inhabited by every sort of suffering imaginable.

It seemed like we were on the edge of a high plain that suddenly opened into an abyss.

Caves and caverns stretched out for miles ahead of us, as if we were standing before the immense crater of a live volcano fed by human suffering, because inside it vortexes of voices exploded continuously like a strange mixture of human and animal cries.

I trembled in my innermost fibers. Both Eloi and I instinctively wanted to flee.

The Instructor, however, remained firm.

Rather than endorsing our weakness, he deliberately ignored it and said calmly:

"Here, as if they were withered branches, there are thousands and thousands of souls who abused the sacred gifts of life. They are defendants in the court of their own consciences, personalities who managed to live upon the ruins of their 'self', confined within the dark sector of mental alienation. They are ridding themselves of the poisonous residues they accumulated within themselves over long years devoid of spiritually constructive work in the physical world. Now they are involved in endless days of redemptive torment."

Perhaps because our astonishment continued to grow at the sight of that heartrending, dreadful picture, he added serenely:

"What we are looking at is nothing but the surface of dark prisons that are enmeshed with sub-crustal precipices."

"But isn't there recourse for such destitution?" asked Eloi, wringing his hands.

Gubio thought for a few moments and continued in a grave tone:

"When we find a single dead body, it is easy to give it a proper burial, but if there are multitudes of corpses, there is nothing to do but throw them in a ditch. All spirits are reborn in the physical realm to destroy the idols of lies and darkness, and to enthrone within themselves the principles of victorious sublimation for eternity, if they are not on the simple, evolutionary road; however, in the demonstrations of a higher order – which are their responsibility – they prefer, in most cases, to love death in idleness, in injurious ignorance or in disguised crime, neglecting the glorious immortality that is theirs to achieve. Instead of constructing a sanctifying destiny with the infinite future in mind, they neglect opportunities for growth, run from the healthy learning experience and bring clamorous debts upon themselves, thereby delaying the work of spiritual growth. If they themselves, owners of the precious gifts of intelligence, with a whole heritage of religious revelations at hand to solve the problems of the soul, willingly entrust themselves to such a delay, what can we do but follow the lines of patience by which the influence of our benefactors is regulated? Yes, this landscape is heartrending and disturbing, but it is both comprehensible and necessary."

I asked him if in those purgatorial places there mightn't be any friendly companions with the mission of consolation, to which the Instructor responded in the affirmative.

"Yes," he said, "this immense collectivity, composed of individualities, who, due to continuous suffering, are characterized by sub-human comportment, are not forgotten. Selflessness works hand in hand with Jesus everywhere. Presently, however, we don't have the means to identify the missionaries and servants of the Good. Let's focus on what interests us more closely."

We descended a few meters and found a squalid woman stretched out on the ground.

Gubio looked at her with his lucid eyes, and after some moments, asked us to grasp his accurate remark.

"Can you see it, Andre?" he asked.

I noticed that the wretch was surrounded by three ovoid forms that were different from each other in disposition and color. They would have been imperceptible to my eyes if I hadn't applied all my powers of attention.

"Yes," I replied, curiously, "I can see three living figures juxtaposed on her perispirit, although they seem to express themselves through a type of matter that looks like a light, fluid and amorphous gelatin."

Gubio explained:

"They are unfortunate entities that have wasted precious time on vengeful purposes due to the rebelliousness that torments their being. They have spent their perispirits under unspeakable torments of desperation and they are automatically drawn to the woman they hate, a sister who, in turn, has not yet discovered that the science of love is the science of freedom, illumination and redemption."

We looked at the wretched creature more closely.

Gubio assumed the attitude of a doctor in the presence of patient and interns.

Enveloped in an aura of "dark gray energies," the suffering woman sensed our presence and screamed amid affliction and derangement:

"Joaquin! Where's Joaquin? Please tell me, for God's sake! Where have you taken him? Help me, please help me!"

Our guide comforted her with a few words, but he could not offer her much attention beyond what a psychiatrist would offer to a patient experiencing a grave crisis. He remarked:

"Examine the ovoids! Probe them magnetically with your hands."

I did so immediately.

I touched the first one and noticed that it reacted positively.

I used my will and linked my hearing faculty to the entity's inner field, and by means of the thread of thought, I was amazed to hear cries and phrases as if they were far off:

"Revenge! Revenge! I'll not rest until the end ... This wretched woman shall pay me!"

I repeated the experiment on the other two and the results were identical.

Shouts of "Murderer! Murderer!" poured forth from each one.

After probing the woman to examine her, the Instructor explained:

"Joaquin was her husband, who has preceded her in the endeavors of reincarnation. He has already returned to the physical realm in order to prepare a place for her. The poor thing is waiting for a chance to return to the beneficent struggle. I can see her cruel drama. She was a ruthless slave owner last century.[9] In her mental archives, I can see fond memories of her prosperous and happy plantation. She was young and beautiful, but in keeping with the schedule of redemptive trials, she married an elderly gentleman who had already assumed sentimental commitments to the humble daughter of a slave. Despite the natural change in his life because of the marriage, he did not abandon his debt. Consequently, the poor, still-young, penitent and unhappy slave mother remained bound to the plantation with the children of her unfortunate love affair. As time went by, the inquisitive, possessive wife found out about the affair and revealed the irascibility that filled her soul. She angrily and violently confronted her husband, forcing him to yield to the jealousy that exacerbated her mind. The poor slave was separated from both of her children and sold into an unhealthy region of the country, where she soon met death due to a malignant fever. The wife had the two boys tied to the pole, where they suffered humiliation and whipping in front of the other slaves. Accused

9   The 19th. – Tr.

by the foreman – on orders from the dreadfully selfish woman – of being thieves, the two slaves were forced to wear a heavy chain attached to their bruised necks. They lived in constant humiliation. In just a few months, they died of tuberculosis. Once discarnate, they found their rebellious mother and formed a trouble-making trio on the plantation, nourishing the sinister purposes of revenge. In spite of pleas for tolerance and forgiveness by spirit friends that visited them frequently, they never gave up the dark purposes they had vowed in their hearts. They mercilessly attacked the woman that had inflicted so much pain on them, imposing destructive remorse on her weak and vacillating spirit. In dominating her psychic life, they became her unseen tormenters and made use of every means possible to increase her troubles. As a result, she fell seriously ill but defied all counsel and healing measures. In spite of being helped by various doctors and priests, she never did recover her physical balance and her body wasted away little by little. Incapable of mentally growing towards the lofty idealism that corrects inner aberrations and facilitates the vibrational cooperation of souls that dwell in higher realms, our unfortunate plantation owner suffered ten years of constant and indefinable bitterness, isolated as she was in the destructive pride that marked her pathway. Of course, she had friends who were ready to offer her their benevolent hands at the time of her inevitable death; however, when we are blinded by evil, we are incapable of receiving any resources of the Good."

The Instructor paused briefly and then continued:

"Rid of her physical bonds, she found herself persecuted by her victims of yesteryear, and her ability to move was restrained due to the vibrational emissions of her own disturbing fears. She suffered incredibly, despite the compassion of benefactors from the higher spheres, who continued to try to lead her to humility and renewal through love. But shared hatred is a blazing furnace that keeps one blind and rebellious. Her half-crazy husband discarnated and found her in a state of invincible languor, but was unable to help her due to the suffering of his own difficult redemption. Her ruthless enemies continued their deplorable endeavor, and even after losing their perispirits, they attached themselves to her by means of the principles of mental matter that envelops them. Rebelliousness and fear of the unknown, in addition to an absolute lack of forgiveness, bind them to one another like bronze shackles. In her present situation, the wretch cannot see or touch them, but she senses their presence and hears their voices through the unmistakable acoustics of the conscience. She lives in torment, directionless. She behaves like a nearly irresponsive being."

The wretched creature did not seem to register this information. She was still clamoring for the help of her husband.

I took the opportunity to ask a few questions:

"In light of this moving scene, how are we to view its solution?" I asked.

"We would be wasting our time. The disturbance arrives unexpectedly and takes hold very quickly; however, it wanes very slowly. We will have to await the patient work of time."

After a pause, he continued:

"Everything leads me to believe that missionaries of charity have already led the husband back to the currents of reincarnation, and we can assume that this sister is bound to follow very soon. Of course, she will be reborn into a tormented life and will face immense obstacles in order to meet her ex-husband again and take part in his future experiences. So…"

"Will these enemies be her children?" I asked anxiously, breaking his reticence.

"Yes, they will, and the case is already under superior jurisdiction. This woman will retake a physical body and will be followed by the spirits of her enemies who, with her, will await the time of immersion in the fluids of the earth."

"Oh!" I exclaimed, deeply amazed, "she won't be separated from her persecutors even when she returns? I have seen reincarnations that are invariably planned out according to special measures."

"Yes, Andre," agreed the Instructor, "you saw processes in which great intercessory elements were at work, attending to the noble mission of those with interests in the future, and with divine help, there are millions of such cases. However, in certain sectors of the human struggle, there are millions of rebirths of criminal souls that turn to immersion in the flesh compelled by the Higher Spheres in order to expiate grave wrongs. In cases like that, the individuality responsible for the disharmony becomes the center of gravitation for the imbalanced consciences due to his or her wrong, and he or she assumes command of the endeavors of the long and complex readjustment in accordance with the dictates of the Law."

Grasping my astonishment, Gubio remarked:

"Why so surprised? The principles of attraction govern the entire universe. There are nuclei and satellites in planetary systems, as well as in atomic systems. In the life of the spirit, the essentials are no different. If good spirits represent centers of attention for spirits attuned to their ideas and tendencies, great criminals become magnetic nuclei for minds that have wandered off the upright path in obedience to them. We grow spiritually with those we love and we redeem or debase ourselves with those we persecute and hate."

His statements inspired me with profound thoughts concerning the magnificence of the laws that govern life, and heedful of the thought of that moment, I avoided any more questions.

The Instructor caressed the brow of that unfortunate creature, intentionally enveloping her in a blessing of divine fluids, and added:

"Poor sister! May Heaven strengthen her for the journey she is about to undertake! Closely followed by the influence of the beings bound to her in the mental abyss of hatred, she will have a dolorous and dark childhood due to unknown sorrows that will accumulate, incomprehensively, upon her oppressed soul. She will suffer from illnesses impossible to diagnose for now in the picture of human knowledge, because they will be caused by the persistent and invisible activity of enemies from another time … Her teen years will be tormented by dreams of motherhood and she won't have any respite until, on her lap, she can kiss the three enemies that have become her tender children … She will carry with her three unbalanced centers of life, and until she readjusts them in the forge of sacrifice to lead them back to the upright path, she will, as their mother, be a tormented magnet or the obscure and sad seat of a constellation of pain."

The lesson was profoundly absorbing and fascinating, but time was pressing and we had to head back.

8
Unexpected Intercession

The room where we were received by the priest Gregorio was like a strange sanctuary lit with burning torches.

Seated on a small throne that emphasized his figure within the disagreeable environs, the strange personage was surrounded by more than a hundred spirits in a worshipful posture. Two extravagantly dressed courtiers were swinging large censors burning strong-smelling substances.

Gregorio was wearing a scarlet robe and was shrouded by a dark brown aura, the disturbing and compelling rays of which hurt our eyes.

He looked at us with piercing, inquisitive eyes and extended his right hand, giving us to understand that we could approach.

Highly excited, I followed Gubio.

What was Gregorio's status there in that room? A tyrannical chief or a living icon filled with mysterious power?

Twelve creatures were kneeling humbly on both sides of the golden seat, attentive to his orders.

With a mere gesture, he set the secretive atmosphere for our conversation, for in just a few seconds, the room emptied of the strange figures.

It was clear that we were going to discuss a grave matter and I watched our guide so that I could copy his movements.

Followed closely by Eloi and me, Gubio approached our host, who was contemplating him with an unkind look. I noticed our Instructor's efforts to surmount the present obstacles so as not to make himself a liar in light of his conscience.

Gregorio greeted him with feigned complacency and spoke:

"Remember that I am the judge, the representative of the powerful government established here. Consequently, you must speak the truth."

After a short pause, he added:

"In our first meeting, you uttered a name…"

"Yes," answered Gubio serenely, "that of a benefactor."

"Repeat it!" ordered the priest imperatively.

"Matilde."

Gregorio's countenance turned grave and anguished. One could say that he had been struck by an invisible dagger. Nevertheless, he feigned hard impassibility, and with the firmness of a proud but tormented administrator, he asked:

"What does this person have to do with me?"

Our guide answered, unaffected:

"She told us that she is devoted to you with unveiled motherly love."

"An obvious mistake!" Gregorio concluded angrily. "My mother left me centuries ago. What is more, even if I were interested in meeting her again, we are fundamentally divorced from each other. She serves the Lamb. I serve the Dragons!"[10]

---

10 Spirits that have been lost in evil ever since the beginnings of the Planetary Creation, and who operate in the lower realms of life, personifying the leaders of rebelliousness,

That particularity of the conversation was enough for my curiosity to explode out of control. Who were these dragons? Satanic spirits of legend? Fallen spirits on the evolutionary road, whose minds were turned against the wholesome and redemptive principles of Christ, whom we all worship as the Lamb of God? No, I was not mistaken; however, Gubio looked at me significantly after silently probing my inner questions, and wordlessly invited me to keep my astonished, half-open lips still.

Inarguably, that instant was not appropriate for the conversation of a learner. It was meant for the knowing, sure manifestations of a master.

"Honorable priest," our guide began, to my great surprise, "I cannot question your personal reasons. I know that there is an absolute order in the creation and I am fully aware of the fact that each spirit is a different world and that each conscience follows its own course."

"Are you perchance criticizing the Dragons, those charged with Justice?" asked Gregorio harshly.

"Who am I to judge?" Gubio answered humbly. "I am but a mere servant in the school of life."

"Without them," continued the hierophant somewhat angrily, "what would preserve the earth? How could the love that saves function without the justice that corrects? The Great Judges are feared and condemned; nevertheless, they endure the human garbage; they coexist with the nasty wounds of the planet; they deal with the world's crimes and have become the prison guards of the perverse and vile."

And like a guilty person who goes to great lengths to justify himself, he continued angrily:

---

hatred, pride and selfishness. However, they are not demons for all eternity, because individually they are being transformed for the Good over the course of the centuries, just as human beings are. – Spirit Auth.

"The children of the Lamb may help and even rescue many. However, there are millions of individuals,[11] like myself, who ask for neither help nor liberation. It is said that we are nothing but moral delinquents. So be it. We are criminals watching over one another. The earth belongs to us because animality rules upon it, offering us the ideal atmosphere. I myself have no notion of heaven. It may be a court for the elect. But for us, the world is a vast kingdom for the condemned. In the physical body, we are prey to the web of fatal circumstances; however, the web that the lower realms have prepared for us will serve millions. If our destiny is to separate the wheat from the tares, our sifter will not lie idle. Experienced as we are in the fall, we shall test all those who appear to us on the road. The Great Judges have ordered us to guard the gates. Thus, we have servants everywhere. All men and women that have wandered away from the pathway of normal evolution are subject to us, and you surely know that there are millions of them. Furthermore, earth's tribunals are ineffective at uncovering all the crimes that occur. Yes, we are eyes in the darkness, and the smallest hidden dramas do not go unnoticed by us."

During a pause, I looked at Gubio's face, which showed no signs of alteration. Humbly looking at Gregorio, Gubio continued:

"Great priest, I know that the Supreme Lord uses us in his divine work according to our tendencies and potential for fulfilling his designs. The phagocytes in the human body are used for the elimination of impurities, just as lightning strikes mercilessly to cleanse the atmosphere of imbalances. I respect your power because if the Heavenly Wisdom is aware of the

---

11 We must not forget that this is the argumentation of an intellectually powerful spirit who has not accepted the illumination of Christ. Thus, he is identical to many of the world's individuals obsessed by the follies of the intelligence. – Spirit Auth.

existence of the tender leaves of the trees, it also knows the purpose of your extensive realm; however, wouldn't you agree that our intervention prevails over fatalism, the closed circle of the circumstances that we ourselves create? I am not qualified to appraise the work of the Judges who administer these realms of reparatory suffering … But I do know about the dreadful images that unfold before your eyes. I have seen firsthand the criminals that are drawn to one another and I have at times probed the dark dramas of those who lie in the caves of suffering, held there by the evil they practiced. I also know that Justice must reign according to sovereign determinations. However, respectable Gregorio, don't you think that if love were to dwell in every heart, it would redeem every sin? Don't you perchance believe in the final victory of goodness through the fraternal work that uplifts us and leads us to the Supreme Father? If we were to spend the same energies on divine commitment to the Lamb that we spend on service to the Dragons, wouldn't we reach the objectives of the final triumph much faster?"

Displeased, the priest listened, but then answered in an unpleasant tone of voice:

"How could I have listened to you in silence for so long? We here are judges in the deaths of all those who wasted life's treasures. How can love ever dwell in unruly souls? Didn't the Lamb once say that we should not cast pearls before swine? For each shepherd of the flock on earth, there are a thousand swine bearing the insignias of the flesh. And if your Master is calling shepherds to his ministry, what can we do on our part but gather teams of strong minds who specialize in correcting the morally delinquent creatures that are placed under our guiding rod? The Dragons are the preserving genii of the physical world and they are particularly interested in preserving the agglutination of the planetary elements. In keeping with logic, they do not believe in a paradise that is imposed. If love were to conquer the earth overnight, disintegrating its dark abysses so that the sublime light may easily and instantly shine forever, how could such a climate encompass the consciences of wolves, lions, panthers and tigers (by their extreme resemblance to such wild beasts): souls that inhabit thousands and thousands of human forms? What would Heaven be if we did not watch over hell?"

Thunderous, sarcastic laughter followed his words.

Gubio, however, was not ruffled.

With simplicity, he considered:

"Even so, I must say that, if we all made a real effort to help the miserable, misery would be wiped out; if we would educate the ignorant, there would be no darkness; if we would assist the morally delinquent and encourage them to take up the regenerative struggle, crime would be swept from the face of the earth."

The priest rang a bell, which to me seemed only to heighten his anger. He shouted raucously:

"Shut up, you insolent fool! You know that I can punish you!"

"Yes," agreed our imperturbable guide. "I think I know the extent of your power. At the least order from your lips, I and my companions could receive prison and torture, and if that is your heart's desire, then we are ready. We knew beforehand that the odds were stacked against us in this venture; however, love inspires us and we trust in the same Sovereign Power that allows you to mete out justice."

Faced with such courage, Gregorio stared at Gubio in amazement, and obviously taking advantage of the moment's psychological transformation, Gubio stated with serene firmness:

"Matilde, our benefactor, told us that you have not forsaken your worthiness and that your lofty qualities of character have remained inviolable, in spite of the different direction you have taken. That is why I can discern your personal worth and can address you as 'respectable' in my appeals."

The priest's anger seemed to abate.

"I don't believe you," he said, annoyed, "but be frank about what you want. I don't have time for pointless conversation."

"Venerable Gregorio, I shall be brief," stated our Instructor meekly. "Listen to me with tolerance and kindness. You know that your spiritual mother has never forgotten Margarida, whose is currently threatened needlessly with insanity and death."

Upon hearing this, the hierophant changed visibly and displayed undisguised trouble on his face. The strange aura around his head revealed darker tonalities. A marked hardness could be seen in his cat-like eyes and his lips contracted in a rictus of infinite bitterness.

I got the impression that he would incinerate us if he could, but he remained immovable, in spite of his aggressive expression.

"You are quite aware that Matilde had in your former wife a much-loved pupil. That tormented daughter's prayers have reached Matilde's selfless and enlightened soul. Gregorio: Margarida has undertaken to live in the body, hungry for redemption. Renewing aspirations bathed her childhood and now that she is married in the fullness of her youth, she has strengthened her hopes, desirous of remaining on the beneficent battlefield to redeem her wrongful past. Obviously, you have strong reasons to force her to return to this plane because you have set her on the road to death. I neither reprove nor accuse you, for I am nothing. Even if the Lord were to confer on me such a lofty representative mission, I still would not be able to judge you, except after having experienced your tragedy and your pain. I know, however, that due to love and hatred from the past, she is strongly connected to the rays from your mind, and we all know that, sooner or later, creditors and debtors must meet one another face to face … However, her current existence entails a large-scale work of salvation. She married an old partner of the evolutionary battle who is no stranger to your heart, and she will reign maternally in a home in which devoted benefactors will organize a lovely ministry of illuminative endeavor. Spirit friends of the truth and goodness have been prepared to receive her motherly tenderness, like flowers blessed by heavenly dewdrops on their way to precious fructification. Consequently, I have come to ask you to mitigate your cruel vendetta. Our souls, no matter how impassive, change over time. Time destroys everything, yet it rids us of our entire storehouse of inferiority so that the work of spiritual growth may continue. The matter that serves for our manifestations changes as the days go by. And even if they were invincible, the powerful Judges, whom you obey, could never supersede the sovereign authority of the All-Merciful, who allows them to act in the name of the corrigendum as they carry out their task for the common good."

Heavy minutes of expectation and silence weighed upon us.

Even so, rather than being discouraged, the Instructor began once again in a pleading voice:

"Even if you still cannot harken to the resources interposed by the Law of the Divine Lamb, who urges reciprocal and sanctifying love, do not turn a deaf ear to the appeals of a mother's heart. Help us free Margarida by saving her from destructive persecution. We are not asking for your personal concourse. Your indifference will be enough so that we may work with all the freedom we need.

The hierophant laughed uneasily and remarked:

"I can see that you know what justice is."

"Yes, I do," agreed Gubio sadly.

Our host said shamelessly:

"Those who issue orders are want of self-sacrifice; those who defend order know no forgiveness. The lawgivers portrayed in the Bible determined that judgments had to be based on the principle of exchange: 'An eye for an eye, a tooth for a tooth.' Since you seem so well-informed about Margarida, do you honestly think you can quell the reasons that compel me to decree her death?"

"I am not disputing you motives," said our guide, amid affliction and sadness, "but I would dare insist on my fraternal plea. Help us save that priceless, fruitful life. By helping us, who knows? Perhaps, by means of the loving arms of today's victim, you yourself may return to the lustral cleansing of the human experience and renew your pathway for the glorious future."

"Any idea of returning to the flesh is unthinkable!" shouted Gregorio.

"We know, great priest," continued Gubio calmly, "that due to Margarida's connections with your powerful and active mind, any sort of liberating activity on our part would be very difficult without your permission. Promise us freedom to act! We are not asking you to suspend her sentence, nor do we intend to declare Margarida innocent. Those who assume debts before the Eternal Laws will have to face them now or later in order to pay them off. But we would ask you to postpone the execution of your purposes. Grant your debtor a beneficent reprieve in honor of your mother's devotion. And if possible, time will modify this dolorous process."

With a look of surprise due to the unexpected request for a postponement, when we ourselves were expecting our guide to demand a permanent repeal, Gregorio considered, less scathingly:

"I have need of the psychic nourishment that only Margarida's mind can provide me."

More encouraged, Gubio asked:

"But what if you could experience once again the sweet comfort of a mother's tenderness to uphold your soul until Margarida, redeemed and happy, could furnish you with the sublimated bread of the spirit?"

The priest stood up for the first time and said:

"I do not believe…"

"But what if we were to propose such a blessing in exchange for your neutrality regarding our saving efforts? Would you allow us to work concomitantly with the servants who obey your orders? Would you keep from inciting them against us and let us work alongside them as we attempt the restoration? In that way, time would add the finishing touches to your decisions."

Gregorio reflected for a moment, and replied:

"It's too late."

"Why's that?" asked our Instructor uneasily.

"Margarida's case," explained the hierophant in a significant tone, "is in the hands of a phalanx of sixty of my skillful servants. They are under the command of a ruthless persecutor who hates her family. The whole matter could be resolved in just a few hours, but I do not want her to return to my arms with the rebelliousness of a victim, in whose inner fount I could only gather the turbulent waters of despair and bitterness. She is to be tormented just as she tormented me in another time; she will suffer nameless humiliations and she will regard death as an asset. Smitten by such suffering, her mind will receive me as a loving and providential benefactor, and she will envelop me in waves of affection, for which I have been waiting for many years … Any attempt to liberate her would be fruitless. Her ability to reason is being disturbed and the magnetization work of drawing her to her death is almost concluded."

Our guide, however, was not to be defeated, and insisted:

"What if we were to become part of your phalanx to attempt the work we are proposing? We would attend to the sick woman as your friends, and without disrespecting your authority, we would try to carry out the plan that brought us here, bearing witness to the humility and the love that the Lamb teaches us."

Gregorio thought for a long while in silence, but Gubio continued with simplicity and firmness.

"Grant it! … Grant it! … Give us your word as a priest! Remember that, someday, you will meet your mother again, even if you don't think you will!"

After long minutes of reflection, the priest raised his arms and said:

"I do not think your attempt will be successful; nonetheless, I will go along with it. I will not interfere."

Then, Gregorio rang the bell and told his servants to approach. As if semi-defeated in a battle against his own conscience, he called for a certain Timao, who appeared in front of us with the look of an executioner. Gregorio asked him about the "Margarida case" and was told that the process of mental alienation was almost finished. It was a matter of just a few days before she would have to be put in a hospital.

Somewhat constrained, Gregorio pointed to us and ordered the sinister attendant to place us in the phalanx that was actively carrying out the gradual execution of her death sentence.

9
Invisible Persecutors

The next morning, we went with some ignorant, misguided spirits to a comfortable residence, where an unexpected scene was about to greet us.

The dwelling denoted the aristocratic status of its occupants, not only by its very large size but also by the magnificent grounds that surrounded it. We stopped in front of the left wing and I could see that it was occupied by a number of pitiable spirit personalities.

Criminal, sinister faces.

Judging by their dark auras, there could be no doubt that the place was being watched over by cold, impassive prison guards.

I crossed the threshold with a heavy soul.

The air was saturated with noxious elements. I did my best to hide my discomfort as I gathered troubling and dolorous impressions.

A large group of low order spirits came into the entryway to probe our intentions. However, following our guide's instructions, we did everything we could to make ourselves look like common criminals. I noticed that Gubio himself had made his perispirit so dark, so opaque, that if we had not been with him from the start, we would not have recognized him.

A merry, bad-mannered fellow named Sergio introduced us to Saldanha, the head guard.

He greeted in a hostile manner, but when we said the password that Gregorio had given us, he accepted us as if we were important comrades.

"So, the boss has decided to torment her a bit more?" Saldanha asked the Instructor confidentially."

"Yes, he did," Gubio stated vaguely, "but we would like to examine the patient as well as the overall conditions."

"The young woman is slowly getting weaker," explained the odd character as he led us down a long corridor permeated with detestable fluidic substances.

He accompanied us somewhat graciously but distrustfully, and after a short pause, he left us alone at the door of a large bedroom.

It was a bright morning outside and the sun was visiting the room through a crystalline window.

A young woman, displaying extreme paleness on the noble lines of her face, was thinking troubled thoughts.

I could tell that this was Margarida, the obsessed woman that our guide meant to help.

Two dreadful-looking discarnates were bent over the patient's chest area, confident and domineering, subjecting her to a complex magnetic operation. That particularity of the scene was bad enough, but my fear grew even worse when I concentrated all my powers of attention on the smitten woman's head. Interpenetrating the thick matter of the bed where she was lying, there were a few dozen "ovoid bodies" of various sizes and of a lead-like color. They looked like large, living seeds connected to the patient's brain via very fine threads carefully arranged along the medulla oblongata.

The discarnate persecutors' work was meticulous, cruel.

Through her perispirit, Margarida lay completely bound, not only to her truculent persecutors, but also to the large group of unconscious entities, which, in accordance with the character of their mental vehicle, were vampirizing her energies.

Actually, I had observed a large number of cases of violent obsession before, but they were always controlled by fulminating passions. Here, however, the assault was technically organized.

It was obvious that the "ovoid forms" had been brought in by the hypnotizers that were controlling the picture.

With due permission, I analyzed the patient's violated physical area. I could see that all her metabolic centers were being controlled. Even her blood pressure was under the influence of the persecutors. The thoracic area displayed appreciable sores on the skin, and upon examining them closely, I saw that the patient was inhaling dark substances that not only weighed upon her lungs but which were reflected especially in the cells and fibers, forming ulcerations on the epidermis.

The vampirization was incessant. The normal energies of the body seemed like they were being transported to the "ovoid forms," which were mechanistically feeding on them with an indefinable sucking movement.

I lamented the fact that it was impossible to consult the Instructor, because had Gubio been free to, he would have explained things in detail; but I concluded that the poor woman must have been attached through the central nervous system, since, judging by the slow destruction of the nerve fibers and cells the sinister purposes of the persecutors were obvious.

Margarida was exhausted and embittered.

With the vestibulocochlear (nerve responsible for bodily balance)[12] in the cerebellum controlled and the optic nerves enveloped by the hypnotizers' influence, her frightened eyes gave an idea of the hallucinatory phenomena that assailed her mind, allowing us to perceive the low level of the visions and auditions to which she was being subjected.

I discontinued my detailed observations in order to examine the psychological posture of our guide, who had run the risk of helping that sick woman whom he loved as a very dear daughter.

Gubio was struggling not to betray the immense pity that dominated him before that patient being led to her death.

In my human condition, I realized that if the patient were that dear to me, I would not hesitate one second to apply liberating passes along the medulla oblongata to relieve her of that heavy, useless, sickly mental burden. Then, I would fight her persecutors one by one.

But our Instructor did not proceed like that.

Gubio looked at the heartrending scene with obvious sadness, but then he immediately turned his kindly gaze to Saldanha, as if to ask him for his expert opinion.

Not realizing he was being touched by our guide's positive impulse, the leader of the torture operation felt obligated to offer him some spontaneous information.

"We have been hard at work for exactly ten days," he began resolutely. "The prey was caught completely off-guard, and fortunately, she offered no resistance whatsoever. If you have come to help us out, I can tell you that I don't think there is

---

12 This nerve is part of the vestibular system, connected with structures in the inner ear, which is responsible for the senses of balance and position of the body (Dr. Sonia Doi of the Medical Spiritist Association). – Tr.

much more work to do. A few more days and we'll be able to finish things up."

In my opinion, Gubio already knew all the particulars of the matter, but obviously to win Saldanha's trust, he asked:

"What about the husband?"

"Ah!" Saldanha exclaimed with a scornful smile, "That miserable wretch doesn't have the least notion of what a moral life is. He's not a bad man, but getting married made him go from being an 'enjoyer of life' to being a 'serious man.' Fatherhood would be a millstone for him, and children – if he had any – would be mere playthings. Today he's going to take his wife to church."

And reinforcing his sarcastic tone, he added:

"They're going to mass in the hopes of making things better."

Saldanha had barely finished when a sad, kindly-looking gentleman entered. His loving expression revealed right away that he was the victim's husband. He exchanged loving and comforting words with her and then helped her get dressed.

After a few minutes, I was amused to see that the couple, accompanied by the band of persecutors, took a taxi and headed for a Catholic church.

We followed.

To my mind, the taxi was like a Carnival party car. Several spirits occupied it both inside and out, from the fenders to the shiny roof.

My curiosity was enormous.

When we entered the elaborate church, I witnessed a strange spectacle. There were perhaps five times more discarnates than flesh-and-blood believers there – a complete imbalance. I soon realized that most of them were there for the deliberate purpose of troubling and deceiving the incarnates.

Saldanha was too preoccupied with the victims to pay much attention to us, and Gubio intentionally took us aside in order to explain some things.

We went into the sanctuary, in which there were no less than seven or eight hundred people.

The racket raised by the ignorant and trouble-making discarnates was deafening. The atmosphere was heavy, which made it hard for me to breathe because of the abundant semi-materialized fluids. However, when I looked at the altars, a comforting surprise soothed my heart. The paraments and objects of worship emitted a soft light that radiated up to the sun-lit ceiling of the nave. There was a perceptible, clear dividing line between the energies in the lower part of the sanctuary and those of the upper. The fluids separated like crystalline water and impure oil in a large container.

As I contemplated the lovely light of the niches, I asked our Instructor:

"What are we looking at? Doesn't the second commandment of Moses say that man shall not make graven images to represent the Heavenly Fatherhood?"

"Yes," Gubio agreed, "and the Testament declares than none shall bow down before them. In fact, Andre, it is an error to create idols of clay or stone to symbolize the greatness of the Lord, when our primordial obligation is to worship him in our own consciences. Even so, the Divine Goodness is infinite and here we find ourselves amongst an appreciable number of child-like minds."

And smiling, he added:

"How often, my friend, do children play with dolls in order to prepare themselves appropriately for the responsibilities of adulthood? There are still primitive tribes that worship the Father in the voice of the thunder, and there are tribes that make various animals the object of idolatry. Nevertheless, the Lord does not turn a deaf ear. He uses the elevated impulses they offer him to help them with their educational necessities. In this house of prayer, the altars receive the projections of believers' sublimated mental matter. For almost a century, the fervent prayers of thousands of them have enveloped the niches and articles of worship. It is only natural that they glow. Heavenly messengers use such matter to distribute spiritual gifts to all those who are in tune with the higher realms. The light we offer to heaven always serves as a basis for the manifestations of heaven on the earth."

During a brief pause, I turned my attention to the well-dressed congregation.

Nearly all of them – even those who held delicate objects of worship in their hands – were mentally far removed from the true worship of the Divinity. Their vital auras were composed of colors of a low vibrational level. Dark brown and gray dominated most of them. In a few, black-red denoted vengeful anger, which they could not hide from us. Discarnates in deplorable situations were scattered throughout, displaying the same characteristics.

I realized that the well-dressed believers – even those who wished to pray with sincerity – would have to put forth an immense effort.

The liturgy announced the start of the worship service, but much to my amazement, despite proceeding in their prideful vestments towards the area of light around the high altar, the priest and acolytes were enveloped in shadow, as were the assistants. Nevertheless, three high order spirits from the higher realms became visible on the holy table with the obvious purpose of sowing the divine gifts there. They magnetized the water, saturating it with wholesome and vitalizing energies – just as occurs during Christian Spiritist meetings – and then they applied beneficent fluids to the communion wafers, transmitting their sacred energies to the fine contexture.

Amazed, I returned to observing the congregation, but neither the incarnates nor the ignorant, discarnate brothers and sisters at work in the church registered the presence of the noble spirit emissaries acting in the name of the Infinite Good.

By means of the auras of many of the people, I could see that a certain number of them were indeed making an effort to improve their mental attitude in prayer. Purplish scintillations, tending toward a wavering glow, appeared here and there; however, maleficent discarnates were purposefully trying to disrupt those who were making an attempt at renewing and reverent faith. Nearby, I fixed my attention on a woman who was following the priest with the obvious desire to receive the heavenly blessing. Her moist eyes and the tenuous rays of light shooting out from her mind spoke of sincere aspiration to the greater life, which at that moment was bathing her devout thought. Nevertheless, upon perceiving her constructive hopes, two bad spirits from the lower realms were trying to distract her attention, and according to what I could tell, they were suggesting unwholesome memories, thereby making her attempt futile.

I looked at Gubio, who explained helpfully:

"The history of demonic spirits attacking the devout of varied hues is basically completely true. Perverted intelligences, incapable of receiving the heavenly gifts, become passive instruments of rebellious intelligences. The latter are interested in keeping the masses ignorant, with lamentable disparagement towards the higher spirituality that governs our destinies. That is why the acquisition of faith requires the most persistent individual effort. Trust in the Good, in addition to the enthusiasm for life that religious light infuses into us, modify our vibrational tonality. We benefit infinitely by immersing our inner energies in the sublimated idealism of the sanctifying faith to which we attach ourselves. Yet, our real task does not entail mere words. A profession of faith is not everything. The experience of the soul in the dense body is fundamentally meant for perfecting the individual. It is by means of the struggles of the pathway that individuals grow, purify themselves and become enlightened. Nonetheless, the tendency of most believers is to avoid conflicts along the way. There are people who, after serving their religious ideal for two years, plan to lie idle for twenty centuries. In all places of worship, the Lord's messengers distribute favors and blessings that are compatible with each one's necessities; however, it is crucial for the heart to be prepared along the lines of merit in order to receive them. Between emission and reception, the need for attunement prevails. Without preparatory effort, the atmosphere for the benefit is impossible. It would be futile for us to immediately impose on primitives a life in a palace built by modern culture. Instead of the chords of our music, they would rather hear the sounds of the wind, and a quiver full of arrows would seem more valuable than our more perfect industrial parks. Thus, for someone to set out on the path toward a superior standing in society, he or she must be polite, educated, good-willed, and open to suggestions of improvement and work."

Gubio looked at the seemingly contrite congregation taking part in the ceremony and emphasized:

"In fact, the Mass is a religious act that is as venerable as any other in which hearts seek to identify with the Divine Watch-care; even so, there are few persons who attend with their spirit effectively inclined towards the assimilation of heavenly assistance. And for the formation of such an inner mood, each believer, besides the work of purifying the sentiments, must also fight against the dispersive and perturbing influence of the discarnates who try to quench his or her fervor.

Gubio continued to lend us invaluable explanations allusive to the rite as the Mass was coming to an end.

The voices of the choir were sending harmonious and lucid vibrations throughout the glowing nave, and I was fascinated to see that several sublime spirits with glorified faces were surrounding the altar when the celebrant raised the chalice after having blessed it.

An intense light flowed from the tabernacle to envelop the elements, but I was surprised to see that, upon raising the sublime offering, the priest extinguished its light with the dark gray rays that he himself was sending out in all directions. Then, as he prepared to distribute the Eucharistic meal to the eleven communicants kneeling humbly at the linen-covered altar, I noticed that the communion wafers on the silver paten were veritable flowers crowned with sweet splendor. They were radiating light with such power that the dark magnetism of the priest's hands could not extinguish it. However, when placed on the tongue that was to receive the symbolic bread, the wafer turned black as if by magic. Only one young woman, whose contrition was irreprehensible, received the divine flower with enough purity. I watched the wafer, like a flake of luminescent fluids, pass down the pharynx to shed its light throughout the heart area.

I was intrigued and the thoughtful Instructor explained:

"Have you grasped the lesson? In spite of having been ordained, the celebrant is an atheist and pleaser of the senses. He has made no effort at his own inner sublimation. His mind is far from the altar. He is highly interested in ending the ceremony as quickly as possible so that he does not miss out on a pleasurable trip. As for those who have come to the Eucharistic table filled with contemptible and dark sentiments, they themselves have annulled the undeserved heavenly gift. There is a large number of so-called believers here, but very few friends of Christ and servants of the Good.

The "Go, the Mass is ended" dismissed the faithful, who, at the end of the service, were more like a flock of noisy, beautifully feathered birds.

Absorbed in deep thought in light of what I had just observed, I went with our guide and Eloi to join our patient and her husband as they left for home surrounded by the same band of wretched spirits without the least change.

10
A Learning Experience

When we arrived back at Margarida's home, I was extremely surprised by the fact that our Instructor did not do anything to defend the dear patient.

Exhausted, the young woman went back to bed and gazed blankly into space, absorbed by an indefinable dread.

On Saldanha's cue, one of the unfeeling magnetizers began applying disturbing energies over her eyes to irritate the support tissue. Not only did the lenses of both her visual organs register hallucinatory phenomena, but the ocular arteries also displayed obvious modifications.

Once more I saw how easy it was for perverse spirits of the darkness to hypnotize their victims, imposing psychic torment on them in any way they pleased.

Tears bathed the patient's face, revealing her inner troubles.

Dilacerated, her afflicted and suffering mind tyrannized her rapidly beating heart, causing grave alterations throughout the organic cosmos.

After completing the complex operations on her eyes, the magnetizer turned his attention to the vestibulocochlear nerve and the auditory cells, infusing them with a dark substance, as if he were filling a gas tank.

Even if she wanted to, Margarida would not have been able to get up. A thick emission of toxic fluids was mixing in with the lymph in the semi-circular canals.

Once this weird procedure had ended, Saldanha dismissed his dreadful collaborators – except for the two in charge of the hypnotic work – telling them they had work to do in another part of town. Other cases were waiting for Gregorio's legion, and in the head tormenter's opinion, Margarida had received enough prostrating matter for the next thirty hours.

The house emptied out little by little so that it now resembled a nest bereft of its voracious hornets. Saldanha, the two magnetizers and the three of us remained behind, along with the group of minds in "ovoid form," which were attached to the tormented woman's brain.

Alone with the fearsome obsessor, Gubio tried to discretely probe his soul.

"There can be no doubt that your faithfulness to your commitments is very admirable," stated our guide.

And as Saldanha smiled at the flattery, Gubio continued with a penetrating yet gentle look:

"What led Gregorio to entrust such a delicate mission to you?"

"Hatred, my friend, hatred!"

"For her?" asked Gubio, nodding toward to the patient.

"Not for her personally, but for her father, a soulless judge who wrecked my home. Exactly eleven years ago, his cruel sentence fell upon my descendants and destroyed them."

And because of our Instructor's look of genuine interest, the wretch continued.

"In rebellion against my extreme poverty and overcome by rampant tuberculosis, I abandoned my physical body but was unable to leave my home environment. My poor Iracema had left me a dear son, to whom I was not able to bequeath any appreciable resources. Consequently, Jorge and his mother were faced with difficulties and afflictions that I cannot recall without immense anguish. Jorge worked as a laborer but could not support them well enough. His mom languished silently in continuous suffering. Even so, Jorge got married when still quite young to a coworker, who gave him a tormented and suffering little daughter. Life was going on as usual for that undernourished and unprotected home, when a certain crime involving robbery and murder struck the place where my poor boy was working. Due to circumstantial evidence, the guilt fell on him. I went with him to prison, and without any recourse to help him, I watched the infernal interrogation to which he was submitted, as if he were a common murderer. Well, from the moment I attached myself to my family after the awful moment of my corporeal transition, I never felt disposed to submission. The human experience had not provided me with time for religious or philosophical studies. Very early on, I grew accustomed to rebelling against those who enjoy the world's benefits to the detriment of those disfavored by fate, and I when I saw that the grave did not reveal some sort of miraculous realm, I preferred to continue my life in my dingy slum house, where living with Iracema through deep magnetic ties comforted me somewhat ... I witnessed detestable incidents with indescribable horror. I felt humiliated. And as a man who was invisible to incarnates, I visited wardens and departments, authorities and guards, trying to find someone that could help me save

Jorge, who was innocent. I even identified the real criminal, who, even now, enjoys a highly desirable social position, and I did everything I could to rectify the opprobrious process. But nothing worked. My son suffered all sorts of mental and physical atrocities, punished for a crime he didn't even commit. Discouraged because I couldn't get any satisfaction from the prison's interrogators – who managed to coerce outlandish confessions from my son – I went to the judge in charge of the case in the hopes of intervening. Instead of accepting my inspiration inviting him to show justice and mercy, the judge listened to the opinions of influential friends in political circles, who, in their eagerness to pardon the true criminal, were highly interested in an unjust sentence."

Saldanha paused briefly, accenting the expression of his profound rancor, and then continued:

"Words cannot begin to express my suffering. Jorge underwent awful torture, and Irene, my daughter-in-law, overwhelmed by necessity and misfortune, forgot her obligations as a mother and committed suicide to be near my poor son's unhappy spirit. Tormented with grief, my wife discarnated on a cot of poverty and joined the anguished couple. My granddaughter – now a young woman, but threatened by an uncertain future – does the housework in this home, where Margarida's insane brother subtly tries to lead her into grave moral aberration. The judge in charge of the family received my vows of revenge in a dream and placed her here with his own family in an attempt to repair his crime somewhat. Even so, my revenge shall be no less severe."

I was surprised to see that our guide did not attempt any spiritual instruction. Looking at Saldanha sympathetically, he only stated:

"The sowing of pain really is one that afflicts us the most."

Encouraged by the friendly tone of that statement, Saldanha continued: "A lot of people have invited me to make a spiritual transformation, encouraging me to offer a barren forgiveness. But I won't do it. My poor Jorge was unable to resist Irene's dilacerated mental pressure and Iracema's oppressed mental pressure and went mad. He was transferred from his humid prison cell to a miserable asylum, but he is more like a caged animal. Do you think my mind has the means to think about compassion when I haven't received it in return? As long as such scenes are before my eyes, I'm not open to any religious suggestions. I simply face life. The grave only pulls down the wall of the flesh, whereas our sufferings continue as alive and forceful as when we had to bear our box of bones. It was in that state that the priest Gregorio found me and satisfied my innermost longings. He needed someone with a sufficiently hardened soul to preside over the technical withdrawal of this woman. He wants to rob her of her earthly existence slowly, and he has praised my firm spirit. There are almost always have a lot of servants available for rectifying commitments, but it's not easy to find one who has made up his mind to persevere in vengeance till the end with the same hatred as at the beginning. Gregorio saw that I met that requirement and he entrusted the job to me.

Looking angrily around the room, he shouted:

"Everyone here shall pay! Everyone..."

Astonished, I looked at Gubio, who remained unperturbed and silent.

Had it been me, perhaps I would have poured out a long, judgmental commentary regarding the law of love that governs our destinies; I would have emphatically demanded the persecutor to pay attention to the teachings of Jesus, and if possible I would have made him bite his undisciplined and insolent tongue.

The Instructor did not proceed like that, however.

He smiled without saying a word, trying to hide his sadness.

Two or three long minutes passed.

The clock showed 11:45 a.m., when we heard somebody coming.

"It's her doctor," said Saldanha with obvious sarcasm. "He's going to look for lesions and microbes but he won't find any."

Just then, an elderly gentleman entered the room along with Gabriel, the victim's husband.

The doctor approached the patient and kindly offered her some words of encouragement.

Margarida tried to smile but couldn't – she didn't have the strength.

As they were talking, an obviously well-meaning spirit entered. He saw us and showed that he understood our status, because he looked cautiously at us without saying anything. He approached the doctor, as if he were his devoted assistant.

The specialist did not seem deeply interested in the case, but after he had examined Margarida in her troubling torpor, he conversed with the victim's husband superficially. He stated that in his opinion the young woman was obviously under the control of secondary epilepsy, and that in the final analysis, he would get the help of eminent colleagues and submit her to a detailed examination of the cerebro-meningeal injury, followed by the recommended surgery.

Next however, the newly-arrived spirit put its right hand on the doctor's forehead, as if he wanted to transmit some providential help to him.

The doctor was reluctant, but in a few minutes, urged by an outside suggestion that he could not comprehend precisely, he took Gabriel to one of the corners and asked him:

"Why don't you try Spiritism? Lately, I have heard of a few puzzling cases that have been resolved successfully via that kind of psychotherapy…"

And to show that he had not surrendered his scientific approach to religious idealism, he added:

"According to what we now know, hypnotic suggestion is a mysterious, almost unknown power."

The patient's husband willingly received this advice and asked:

"Could you help me out with it?"

The physician hesitated somewhat and replied:

"Well, I don't have many connections with the exponents of the subject, but according to what I believe, there wouldn't be a problem with trying, at least."

He wrote out some prescriptions for drugs and injections, and then got ready to leave as Saldanha, in complete control of the situation, laughed in scorn.

Gubio discussed some matters with the discarnate inquisitor, and then explained to me:

"Andre, we have agreed that you should go with the doctor and make observations. However, come back here in a few hours."

I understood that our guide was giving me an opportunity to gain some new knowledge and I cautiously and contentedly accompanied the troubled specialist.

Away from the place where our Instructor was locked in an odd battle, I approached the personality that was assisting the doctor, and we engaged in a friendly dialog.

The new friend's name was Mauricio. He had been the doctor's assistant as an incarnate. Now he watched over him and assisted him in his professional undertakings.

"All physicians," he asserted, "even if they have a materialistic mind that is impermeable to religious faith, rely on spirit friends who help them. Human health is one of the most valuable of all divine gifts. But when, because of neglect or a lack of discipline, people mistreat it, it is difficult to restore their centers of equilibrium, because everyone knows that the worst deaf person is the one that does not want to hear. However, as for those on the spirit plane who aid human progress, there are always ways to guard the organic harmony so that people's health is not harmed. Of course there are awful errors in medicine and we cannot avoid them. Our assistance cannot surpass the receptive field of those who want to heal others or themselves. Even so, we always act on the side of overall health as far as possible.

And with a deeply significant expression, he exclaimed:

"Ah! If doctors would only pray!"

We arrived at our destination shortly before our incarnate friend.

The residence was a comfortable one, but in spite of the lovely grounds around it, it was overflowing with disagreeable fluids.

The environment in the home was highly troubled.

Mauricio explained without preliminaries:

"We are highly interested in our friend's involvement in the grand questions of the soul in order to improve the woman's infirm mind. That is why, using indirect means, we have led him to books and publications on the matter. Nonetheless, contrary to our desires, not only do middle-class prejudices predominate, but also the pernicious influence that his second wife has on him. A very intelligent man but extremely attached to rewarding his senses, our friend could not stand widowhood. Consequently, five years ago he married a young woman who demands a lot of him, despite his older age. This has given rise to a very serious state of affairs. The first wife discarnated and left behind two boys. She is still attached to the home, which she regards as her exclusive property. No matter how hard we try, we have not yet managed to remove her, because her sons' thoughts are in conflict with their father's and stepmother's and they are constantly inciting her to do something. The mental dual in this home is enormous. No one yields; no one asks for forgiveness and the ongoing spiritual battle has transformed the place into an arena of darkness.

The informant paused, and we could see that, in her striking position of rebelliousness, the discarnate former lady of the house was, in fact, connected to one of her sons, a young man about eighteen years old who was nervously smoking in an easy chair. He was a perfect receptacle for his mother's rebellious mind.

His head was full of troubling and wrongful thoughts.

Highly tenuous magnetic threads connected him to his unfortunate mother.

His hands were doubled into fists and he looked like he was contriving diabolical plans, and despite Mauricio's attempts to help them, neither he nor his jealous mother proved to be capable of receiving his restorative influence.

"I have done all I can," explained my new companion, "to instill lofty spiritual values in this home, but it is a highly resistant arena."

Just then, the doctor came through the door and Mauricio placed his benevolent hand on his forehead to provide him with precise intuition about Margarida's case. The specialist immediately began to ponder the matter that Mauricio suggested, recalling a certain technical publication. It was the only way he could register his spirit friend's thoughts. His efforts proved unsuccessful.

The son attacked his father with caustic accusations for being so late for lunch.

The doctor quickly disconnected his mind from our invisible threads, immersing it in a whirlwind of antagonistic vibrations.

The discarnate wife also approached him in a fury. I watched as she slapped his face, although he did not notice it. Yet, the blood concentrated in the area of the temples and his face displayed undisguised rage. He muttered a few words full of indignation and lost all spiritual contact with us.

Mauricio was insufferably disappointed and said:

"It's always like this. It is very hard for us to approach those whom we plan to help on the physical plane. We are given invaluable opportunities for spiritual accomplishments, such as the one involving Margarida. However, our attempts result in utter frustration. A man educated by means of academic responsibility should, by himself, possess a holy curiosity regarding life and abstain from certain practices entailing the selfish satisfaction of the incarnate experience. However, people usually pursue such satisfaction until they completely wear out their bodies. No matter how much we try to get them to make the invaluable trip from the periphery to the center so that they can conform to the imperatives of the life that awaits them beyond the grave, our efforts are nearly always considered delayable and pointless."

Mauricio smiled enigmatically, and added:

"And we can see that this is a man that has been called by society to heal others."

Meanwhile, the little family gathered around the table and the doctor's second wife really impressed me with her refined aspect. Her makeup was impeccable. Her garb was elegant and sober, and her jewelry was tasteful. Her hairdo harmoniously enhanced the depth of her look; but she was surrounded by a dark gray aura, which betrayed how little she had grown spiritually. Socially speaking, she seemed to be very refined, but when they had finished eating, she gave evidence of her deplorable mental condition. After an unfortunate argument with her husband, the young woman went to take a nap on a large, soft couch.

Mauricio invited me to observe her as she rested, and I was astonished – stunned, even – that I did not see the same physiological traits in her perispirit, which had abandoned her resting body. I did notice a slight similarity but the woman had truly become unrecognizable. Her face looked like it belonged to one of those witches in old children's tales. Her mouth, eyes, nose and ears were somewhat monstrous.

Not even the rebellious first wife had the courage to confront her. She withdrew half scared and tried to hide behind her son.

I remembered the book in which Oscar Wilde tells the story of Dorian Gray's portrait, which would gradually acquire a horrendous visage as the owner changed inwardly due to the practice of evil, and when I looked at Mauricio questioningly, he explained:

"Yes, my friend, Wilde's imagination did not hallucinate. Men and women, with their thoughts, attitudes, words and actions, create within themselves their true spirit form. Each crime, each downfall, leaves horrendous marks on the soul, just as each benevolent action and each worthy thought increases the beauty and perfection of the perispiritual form, within which the real individuality manifests, especially after the death of the dense body. There are people who are attractive and admirable physically, but who are true mental monsters at heart, just as there are deformed and ugly bodies that hide angelic spirits of celestial beauty."

And nodding toward the unfortunate woman as she was leaving the house partially free of her physical body, he added:

"This poor sister is under the control of scoffing, animalistic spirits who will keep her terribly imbalanced for a long time to come. Unless she acquires a renewing faith, sanctifying ideas and worthy behavior, we don't think she will be able to avoid the peril she's in, and will only remember to weep, learn and dedicate herself to the Good when she finally leaves the physical vessel, which is truly witch-like for now.

The matter was really fascinating and the lesson truly valuable. Unfortunately, I was out of time.

I had to get back.

11
An Invaluable Experience

Heeding of the doctor's suggestion, the next morning Gabriel got ready to take his wife to be examined by a famous professor of psychic sciences in hopes of securing his beneficent help.

I could see that people's freedom regarding such consultations was almost unlimited, because Gubio was not at all pleased about it and discreetly told me that he was going to do everything he could to prevent it; that, in his opinion, it would only be profitable and worthwhile if they went to a different authority on the matter.

In our cautious guide's opinion, the professor was, indeed, an admirable exponent of phenomena, a bearer of remarkable mediumistic gifts, but because his mind was too attached to the common interests of the earthly experience, he could not truly help those who came to him.

"Psychic work," the Instructor said in a nearly imperceptible voice, "is an activity that is as common as any other. The main thing is to develop a sanctifying work. Consulting intermediaries – that is, holders of outstanding faculties in the informative sector – of acknowledged competence when dealing with the two worlds is like contacting holders of great wealth. If holders of such great assets are not interested in using them for the happiness of others, such knowledge or money will only increase their debt of selfishness, useless distraction or the regrettable waste of time."

In spite of this opportune remark, we saw that the obsessed woman's husband was not open to our changing his mind.

All our subtle efforts to get him to take a different course failed. Gabriel did not know how to reflect.

Although visibly worried, Gubio said:

"At any rate, we are here to help and serve in any way we can. Let's follow the couple on this new adventure."

We would soon be meeting the psychiatrist.

With a lot of interest, as if he had known beforehand about what was going to happen, Saldanha followed the tiniest measures without releasing the young woman.

A few minutes before 11:00 a.m., we found ourselves in a large waiting room, waiting to be called in.

There were three other groups of people waiting anxiously.

The professor was in his office treating a mental patient whom we could hear uttering disconnected sentences in a loud voice.

I could see that all those present were accompanied by a large number of discarnates. To be more precise, the whole place was like a large hive of workers without physical bodies.

Low order spirits were coming and going, paying little attention to us.

In light of Saldanha's iron intention to keep Margarida under his strict control, our Instructor said that he wanted to check out the place and took us with him to study some of the other patients.

We approached an older gentleman in an easy chair. He was accompanied by two young men and showed symptoms of an obvious nervous condition. His very pale forehead was covered in cold sweat and lines of dread, displaying his lipothymy. One could see that he was being tormented by fearful visions known only to himself. I perceived his mental troubles and was astonished to see several dark ovoid forms, all different from one another, clinging to his perispirit. I was interested in what our Instructor might have to say. Gubio was studying him meticulously, obviously preparing to offer us invaluable insights. After a few moments, he explained in a muffled voice:

"Notice what physiological calamities mental disturbances can cause a person. This man is a police investigator with serious mental problems. He couldn't hold the 'billy-club' of responsibility. He used it to humiliate and hurt others. He managed to avoid remorse for a few years, but each thought of indignation by his victims began to circle in his psychic atmosphere waiting for a chance to make itself felt. His cruel ways attracted not only the anger of a lot of people but also the constant company of the worst kinds of entities, who ruined his mental life. When the time came for him to look back on his life in the intimacy of the early symptoms of bodily old age, remorse opened a huge breach in the fortress in which he had become entrenched. The accumulated energies of the destructive thoughts he had brought on himself due to his thoughtless conduct were suddenly unleashed through affliction and fear, breaking down his delusive organic resistance, like furious storms that demolish the fragile dam that is supposed to hold back the increasing surge of the waters. Surviving the crisis, imbalanced energies of his troubled mind whip the delicate organs of his physical body.

The most vulnerable ones have suffered terrible consequences. Not only does his nervous system suffer incredible torture but his traumatized liver is on the brink of fatal cirrhosis."

Sensing our silent questions regarding a possible solution for the dolorous enigma, Gubio emphasized:

"Down deep, this friend is actually being persecuted by himself. He is tormented by what he has been and by what he has done. Only an extreme mental change for the Good will keep him in his physical vessel; a renewing faith, along with an effort at persistent and worthy reform to a nobler moral life will confer higher directives on him, providing him with the power needed for self-restoration. He is controlled by the malignant images that he has constructed in isolated and dark rooms through the simple love of mauling unfortunate people under the pretext of safeguarding social harmony. The memory is a living, miraculous photographic plate that holds the images of our actions and gathers the sounds of what we say and hear ... It is with our memories that we either condemn or absolve ourselves."

The subject was alluring, but perhaps not to awaken too much attention from Saldanha and the other uneducated spirits that were eyeing us curiously, Gubio began to study another case with us.

We approached a sofa on which a respectable-looking woman was sitting beside a young chlorotic[13] one. They appeared to be grandmother and granddaughter. Two sinister-looking spirits flanked the girl, as if she were being shielded by over-protective bodyguards.

The older woman was anxiously waiting for a consultation. The girl was talking nonsense, but it was not of her own doing:

---

13 Iron deficiency anemia due to dietary causes (www.bioportal.bioontology.org) – Tr.

tenuous threads of magnetic energy connected her brain to the head of the wretched brother on her left. She was completely controlled by his thoughts, like hypnotist and subject. The girl was smiling blankly and was chatting aimlessly about plans for vengeance with all the characteristics of mental impairment and unawareness.

Gubio examined her with his usual care and then explained:

"This case involves a dolorous drama from the past. Life cannot be seen within the narrow scope of a single physical existence. It encompasses eternity – centuries *ad infinitum*. This girl went into serious debt in the past. She married a man and lured his brother into corruption. The former committed suicide and the latter went mad. Now, here they are, at her side to get their revenge. Her grandmother has set her up to get married because she's afraid to leave her to herself in the world; however, before this beneficent plan can materialize, both victims from her past life are determined to prevent the marriage. The outraged former husband, still in the early stages of his spiritual evolution, cannot forget the wrong she did him; thus, he has taken over her centers of speech and equilibrium. He fills her mind with his own ideas, subjugating her and demanding her presence in his own realm. The poor thing is saturated with fluids that are not her own. She has already consulted several psychiatrists without results; now she has come here seeking help.

"Will she find a suitable remedy?" asked a strongly-impressed Eloi.

"It doesn't look like she's on the right track. She needs inner renewal, and from what I can tell, she will receive only a mild palliative here. In cases of obsession like this one, where the victim can still defend herself, personal resistance is imperative. But it does no good to remove the iron filings that stick to a magnet when the magnet itself continues to attract the filings."

We would have been greatly blessed with more insights if we had continued with this particular case; however, Saldanha was looking at us questioningly and we had to move on.

We came to the darkest corner of the waiting room, where two middle-aged men sat in silence. Right away we could see that one of them was definitely imbalanced. He was very pale and nervous, displaying signs of profound anxiety.

Next to them was a humble-looking discarnate. I took him to be just part of the large group of troubled spirits at work there, but I was pleasantly surprised when he addressed Gubio, exclaiming discreetly:

"I can see by your vibrational tone that you are friends of the Good."

Indicating the patient, he said:

"I have come here on behalf of this friend. As you know, in that office is a powerful medium that has not received inner illumination. He has attracted a few dozen barely educated discarnates, who absorb his emanations and work blindly under his orders, whether good or bad.

He smiled and added:

"Here, patients are not actually helped by the helper himself; instead, they are helped by the spiritually constructive assistance that he has access to."

I asked him about this particular patient and he explained kindly:

"This friend is an austere public administrator. As a steward and discipliner, he cannot use the cotton of tenderness on others' injuries and is subject to needless hatred and silent persecutions that have ceaselessly lashed his mind for many years. This has resulted in perilous reactions in his circulatory system, the area that is the least resistant in his physical cosmos. Struggling fearlessly to readjust the attitudes of lazy employees, but lacking weapons of love for his own defense, his coronary arteries have suffered considerable damage. Similar attacks by imponderable forces have also taken aim at his liver and spleen, which are in a dreadful state. Moreover, the large group of persecutors that were awakened by his forceful and educative work have managed to instill in his doctors the idea of removing his gall bladder. The operation would encounter complications that would cause the unexpected death of his body. The plan is impressively well thought out. Nevertheless, due to the goodness that exists at the bottom of his severity, we are going to try to assist him through this medium. I have received orders to prevent the surgery and I am confident that I will be successful."

Of course, I would have loved to examine the patient to see how much mental damage he had sustained, but a look from Gubio changed my mind.

We had important responsibilities and had to get back to Saldanha. Margarida's case was complex and we had to remain firm to find a solution.

Sensing our willingness to help, the poor woman's obsessor welcomed us trustingly.

Putting on airs of a super-intelligent person, he told our Instructor that he had decided to solicit the neutrality of the professor's spirit helpers. He said, shrewdly, that it was necessary to hamper the medium's compassion and to confuse his examination by every means possible.

After this surprising statement, he ordered one of his most influential collaborators to appear and the odd figure of a dwarf with an enigmatic and expressive face appeared before us.

Saldanha asked for his help, explaining that the psychiatrist was not to get involved with Margarida's problem. In exchange for this favor, he promised excellent remuneration in a nearby colony not only for the dwarf himself but for the other assistants as well. He told him how he would provide him with luxury and pleasures in the hive of perturbed and ignorant spirits where we had met Gregorio.

The dwarf displayed undisguised happiness and assured Saldanha that the medium would perceive nothing at all.

With understandable curiosity, I followed the chain of events.

As soon as we entered the office, I could see that it did not inspire much confidence.

The professor immediately explained his fee and asked Gabriel for a rather large payment up front. The business between the two spheres was like any other negotiation.

I could see right away that even if the medium was able to somewhat control the spirits that used his efforts, by the same token he was easily controlled by them.

The office was full of low order spirits.

Saldanha got right to work and told us that he was going to monitor the medium's procedures closely, and he gleefully told us that he had enlisted the help of all the spirits there.

Consequently, the three of us could observe what was happening and learn a valuable lesson.

Visibly satisfied with the financial arrangements, the medium began to concentrate deeply and I noticed a flow of energies emanating from all his pores, but most especially from his mouth, nostrils, ears, and chest area. That force, resembling a fine and subtle vapor, filled the small office, and I saw that the low order spirits who assisted the medium during his incursions on our plane inhaled it deeply, nourishing themselves with it, just as ordinary persons nourish themselves with protein, carbohydrates and vitamins.

Examining the scene, Gubio explained in a voice imperceptible to everyone else:

"That energy is not the patrimony of the privileged few. It is something common to all individuals, but only those who exert it through precise thinking can understand and utilize it. It is Newton's 'spiritus subtilissimus,' Mesmer's 'magnetic fluid' and van Reichenbach's 'odic force.' In essence, it is a plastic energy of the mind, which accumulates it within itself after having taken it from the universal fluid in which all the currents of life are bathed and renewed in the highly diverse kingdoms of nature within the universe. Each living being is a transformer of this energy, according to that being's receptive and radiating potential. Human beings reincarnate hundreds of times to learn how to use, develop, enrich, sublimate, ennoble and divinize it. However, in most cases, they avoid the struggle, which they interpret as suffering and affliction, when actually it is an inestimable resource for spiritual growth. Thus, they delay their own sanctification, the only way we can draw nearer to the Creator."

Observing the scene that was developing, I commented:

"But, we have to admit that this seeing medium is a powerful instrument. He is in full contact with the spirits that assist him, and who, in turn, find him to be a solid support."

"You're right about that," confirmed our guide serenely, "but there's no indication that he is morally evolved. The professor of relations with our sphere – a sphere that is unapproachable to the ordinary person for now – is attuned to the vibrational emissions of the low order spirits around him, and he can hear their opinions and register their suggestions. But that's not enough. Those who disengage themselves from their corporeal vehicle don't suddenly initiate themselves into divinity. There are billions of evolving spirits surrounding incarnates in every area of struggle. Many of them are of a lower order than their incarnate counterparts are and they easily become passive instruments of incarnates' desires and passions. Hence, a capacity for sublimation is imperative for all those who dedicate themselves to the interchange between the two worlds, for if virtue is transmissible, vices are highly contagious."

Meanwhile, we saw that the medium had disconnected from his body and was listening to the argumentation of the highly intelligent spirit whose cooperation Saldanha had won.

"Go back, my friend," the spirit was saying vaingloriously to the medium, "and tell our sick sister's husband that her organic case is simple and that all she really needs is a doctor's help."

"But isn't she a victim of plain old obsession?" asked the medium somewhat hesitantly.

"No, no; that's not it at all! Make it clear to him that the problem is medically related. Her nervous system is in tatters. She needs shock-therapy in a hospital. That's all."

"But wouldn't it be best to try to do something to help her?!" asked the medium, worried.

The spirit laughed, as if there were no need for concern, and replied:

"Now, now. You should know by now that everyone has their own destiny. If our assistance is to be effective, there's no time for quibbling. Get on with it."

At this point Saldanha smiled in satisfaction, approving the suggestion and showing us that a lot of people can be fooled when they trust only in the narrowness of their own observations.

In light of the situation, I asked Gubio discretely:

"Isn't this an authentic spirit manifestation?"

"Yes, it is," he confirmed gravely, "it is indeed an authentic phenomenon in which an incarnate individuality receives the opinions of a discarnate one. However, Andre, incarnate friends of the Christian ideal are now realizing that such phenomena per se are as rebellious as a mighty river flowing randomly out of control. We will never condone dogmatic, intolerant Spiritism. However, it is essential that a climate of prayer, edifying self-denial, willingness to serve and renewing faith through empowering moral standards comprise the fundamental mark of our transforming mediumistic activities so that we may truly take part in a noble endeavor for the Supreme Father. This man is a medium with rich and broad potential, but who, because of the ordinary business dealings to which he lowered his faculties, he does not awaken constructive impressions in those who come to him. He may be considered a valuable coworker in certain cases, but he is not the ideal collaborator that can elicit the interest of the great benefactors of the Superior Life. Such spirits would not compromise grand teachings by means of otherwise well-intentioned servants who do not hesitate to sell their divine goods for money. The pathway of prayer and sacrifice is thus indispensable to all those who intend to dignify life. A heartfelt prayer increases the radiating powers of the mind, expanding and ennobling its energies, while selflessness and kindness enlighten all those who draw near to their source, which is rooted in the Highest Good. Consequently, it is not enough to merely exteriorize and mobilize the mental force that we all possess; above all else, we must give it a divine direction. That is why we strive for Jesus-centered Spiritism – it is the only way we can keep from going disastrously astray."

I grasped the Instructor's muffled, invaluable explanations, and highly impressed, I kept quiet out of respect.

The medium returned to his physical cage, thereby ending the technical-mechanical contact with our sphere without any result regarding any spiritual elevation that might have improved the environment. He opened his eyes, readjusted himself in his chair and told Gabriel that his wife's problem could be solved with the help of psychiatry. He commented on the precarious condition of her nerves and even recommended a specialist he knew, who would take a different approach to a cure.

The couple gratefully thanked him, and as they said goodbye, the professor advised Margarida to be courageous and cautious whenever she felt depressed.

The young woman listened to these remarks with the disenchantment and pain of someone who felt like the target of sarcasm, and left.

Saldanha congratulated his assistants in the deplorable endeavor and invited them to a get-together to celebrate their triumph. Then, he told us in a firm voice:

"Let's go, my friends! He who plots revenge must follow it through to the end!"

Gubio smiled sadly at him to hide his extreme affliction and we meekly followed him out.

12
A Mission of Love

We went back to the couple's home, where we waited expectantly. Meanwhile, in the middle of the night, Saldanha told us he was going to visit his son in the hospital.

I was shocked when our Instructor asked Saldanha if we could go with him.

Margarida's persecutor was somewhat surprised too. He agreed but wanted to know why.

"Maybe we can be of some help," Gubio responded optimistically.

Saldanha took strict precautions and told Leoncio, one of the two implacable hypnotizers, to stand in for him while we were at the hospital.

Among the many victims of dementia undergoing cruel readjustment, Jorge's situation was truly heartbreaking. We found him lying face-down on the cold cement of his primitive cell. His unmoving face was resting on his wound-covered hands.

The father, who until that moment had seemed impermeable and hardened, looked at his son with visible anguish in his tear-filled eyes and explained with infinite bitterness in his voice:

"He is obviously resting after one of his fits."

Jorge's insanity and anguish was not the only situation that inspired compassion, however. Right next to him, connected to his vital circle, his discarnate mother and wife were absorbing his organic resources. They, too, were stretched out on the floor, semi-lethargic, as if they were experiencing awful pain.

Irene, a suicide, was holding her right hand to her throat – the perfect picture of someone experiencing the dolorous effects of having poisoned herself – whereas her mother was embracing her son, gazing fixedly at him. Both women were displaying unmistakable signs of inner torment. Fluids that looked like a viscous blob covered their brains from the top of the spinal cord to the frontal lobes, and were especially heavy around the motor and sensitive areas.

The two women were concentrating on poor Jorge's energies as if he were the sole bridge for communicating with the existence they had left behind, demonstrating their complete dependence on the base interests of the physical life.

"They're crazy," Saldanha said, obviously trying to be agreeable. "They can see me but they neither understand nor recognize me. They are like children assailed by pain. They had hearts of porcelain that shattered all too easily."

Furrowing his brow in insufferable bitterness, he added:

"Very few women can hold the fort amid the wars of retribution. They usually succumb rather quickly, overcome by useless tenderness."

Wanting to annul our companion's vibrations of anger, our guide cut his destructive statements short, confirming sadly:

"Actually, they are in state of profound hypnosis. Our two sisters here have not yet been able to awaken from the nightmare of suffering in the trance of death. They are like a traveler who is about to cross a raging river without the means needed to reach the other side. In the final moments of their physical bodies, both women focused all their loving concern on Jorge, combining their tortured energies with his, and they appease themselves amid the fluids of their own creation, much like the 'bombyx mori'[14] immobilized and dormant amid the threads that it itself has woven."

Margarida's obsessor grasped these remarks with an undisguised look of surprise, and said more calmly:

"No matter how much I try to make myself known by yelling my name in their ears, they can't hear me. They do moan long, disconnected phrases sometimes, but their memories and awareness seem completely dead. If I insist and carry them away from him, anxiously trying to infuse them with new life so that they can help me carry out our revenge, my efforts are futile, because as soon as I release them they rush back to Jorge, as if they were bits of iron drawn by a powerful magnet."

"Yes, I know," agreed our guide. "They are temporarily crushed by fear, hopelessness and suffering. Due to their lack of continuous, well-coordinated mental effort, they have not been able to expel the 'coagulating energies' of the despondency that they themselves rebelliously caused when faced with the demands of the everyday struggles of earthly life, and they have indifferently caved in to deplorable torpor, in which they feed on Jorge's energies. Constantly drained of his psychic reserves, the patient, hypnotized by both, lives amid hallucinations and despair that are, of course, incomprehensible to those around him."

---

14 Silk worm. – Tr.

With a sincere willingness to serve, Gubio sat down on the cement floor, and in a gesture of extreme compassion, put their heads on his fatherly lap. As the tormenter of the woman he planned to save looked on skittishly, Gubio gave him a kindly look and asked him:

"Saldanha, would you allow me to do something for them?"

The persecutor's face changed.

Judging from the smile that came over his formerly unpleasant and dark look, our guide's spontaneous gesture had disarmed his heart, smiting his innermost fibers.

"Oh yes, please do!" he said almost kindly, "That's what I myself have been trying to do but couldn't."

Highly impressed by the lesson we were receiving, I contemplated the surroundings, comparing them with those of the room where Margarida was going through such affliction and torture. The impediments here were much harder to overcome. The place was filthy. In the adjoining cells, vile-looking spirits were walking around aimlessly. I was amazed to see that a few of them displayed animal-like characteristics. The atmosphere was suffocating, saturated with clouds of dark substances formed by the imbalanced thoughts of the deplorable incarnates and discarnates wandering around.

Faced with such a situation, I asked myself: Since our guide loved Margarida as a spiritual daughter, why hadn't he rendered her such Christian assistance as this? But as I watched the kindness with which our magnanimous mentor was solving the affective problem that was tormenting her adversary, his endeavor gradually enabled me to grasp the thrilling beauty of the gospel teaching: *Love your enemy; pray for those who persecute and slander you; forgive seventy times seven times.*

As we looked on in wonder, Gubio caressed the brows of the three suffering spirits. He seemed to be freeing each one from the heavy fluids that were keeping them benumbed in profound unconsciousness. After about a half hour of stimulating magnetic action, Gubio glanced up at Saldanha, who had been analyzing his tiniest gestures with doubled attention, and asked:

"Saldanha, would you mind if I said a prayer?"

Saldanha looked stunned.

"What?! ... You actually believe in such a panacea?"

But immediately sensing our infinite good will, he said confusedly:

"Well ... OK ... If you want to."

Our Instructor took advantage of that moment of sympathy, and lifting his thoughts to the Higher Realms, he prayed humbly:

Lord Jesus!
Our Divine Friend...
There are always those who pray for the persecuted,
But very few remember to pray for the persecutors!
Wherever we go, we hear prayers
On behalf of those who obey;
But we rarely hear prayers for those who command.
There are many who pray for the weak
So that they may be helped in time;
But few are the souls that implore divine aid for the strong
So that they may be well-guided.
O Lord, your justice never fails.
You know those who wound as well as those who are wounded.
You do not judge according to the standard of our capricious desires,
For your love is perfect and infinite...
You do not incline yourself only
To the blind, the sick and the disheartened,

For, at the right time, you help
Those who cause blindness, infirmity and discouragement...
If it is true that you save the victims of evil,
You also seek out sinners, the unfaithful and the unrighteous.
You did not despise the boastfulness of the doctors of the law,
But talked lovingly with them in the temple of Jerusalem.
You did not condemn the wealthy, but blessed their useful
endeavors.
In the home of Simon, the proud Pharisee,
You did not scorn the wayward woman,
But helped her with your fraternal hands.
You did not forsake evildoers,
But accepted the company of two thieves on the day of the
cross.
If You, O Master,
The Immaculate Messenger,
Proceeded thusly on earth,
Who are we,
Indebted spirits that we are,
To condemn one another?
Light within us the clarity of a new understanding!
Help us see our neighbor's sufferings as our own.
When tormented,
Make us feel the difficulties of those who torment us
So that in your name we may overcome all obstacles.
Merciful Friend,
Do not leave us without guidance,
Relegated to the limitation of our own sentiments...
Help us with our wavering faith,
Disclose to us the common roots of life
So that we may finally understand that we are all brothers
and sisters.

Teach us that, apart from sacrifice,
There is no other law that can enable us evolve
Towards divine worlds.
Enable us to understand our redemptive drama.
Help us to transform hatred into love,
Because in our condition of inferiority,
We only know how to transform love into hatred,
When your will for us changes.
Our hearts are smitten and our feet wounded
On the long journey due to our incomprehension.
And that is why our minds
Aspire to the climes of true peace
With the same affliction
That the weary traveler in the desert
Yearns for pure water.
O Lord,
Infuse us with the gift
Of helping one another.
You helped those who did not believe in you;
You watched over those who did not understand you;
You reappeared to the disciples who forsook you;
You bequeathed the treasure
Of your divine knowledge
To those who forgot and crucified you...
When compared with you,
Why would we,
Miserable worms in the dirt before a celestial star,
Be afraid of extending generous hands
To those who do not yet understand us?!"

The Instructor impressed the last words with a touching tone.

Eloi's and my eyes were full of tears, as were those of Saldanha, who had retreated aghast to one of the dark corners of the depressing cell.

Gubio had gradually transformed himself. The vigorous vibrations of that prayer coming straight from his heart had expelled the darkened substances that he had taken on when we first entered the penal colony and met Gregorio. Sublimated light now shone on the face that the tears of love and compunction had made iridescent with unspeakable beauty. It seemed like he was hiding some unknown light source within his chest and forehead that shot out luminous rays of bright blue. At the same time, a lovely thread of incomprehensible light connected him to the Higher Realms before our bewildered eyes.

After a pause, he intensified the luminosity with which he was enveloping the three persons he was sheltering with his prayer and implored:

It is for these, O Lord,
For these who lie here in thick darkness
That we ask your blessings!
Free them, O Master of light and compassion,
Free them so that they may become balanced and recognize
one another...
Help them
To evolve in the emotions of sanctifying love,
And to abandon the lower passions forever.
May they feel
Your devoted affection,
Because they, too, love you and seek you
Unconsciously
Even though they are being tormented

In the deep valley
Of dark and degrading sentiments...

The Instructor finished. An intense outpouring of light burst forth all around him from hands that were invisible to us. With obvious emotion, Gubio began applying magnetic passes to each of the three wretches, and then said to the incarnate young man:

"On your feet, Jorge! You are now free to expiate your wrongs."

Jorge opened his eyes wide, as if he were waking up from a terrible nightmare. The trouble and sadness had suddenly left his face. In an automatic impulse, he obeyed Gubio's order and stood up in absolute control of his reasoning.

Gubio's measures had broken the ties that had bound him to his discarnate loved ones, liberating his psychic economy.

After witnessing what had happened, Saldanha cried out in tears:

"My son! My son!"

Jorge could not hear his father's enthusiastic exclamations, but went over to the humble cot and lay down in unexpected serenity.

With his highest sentiments won over, Saldanha approached Gubio with the manners of a humbled child that has acknowledged his teacher's superiority; but before he could grasp Gubio's hands to kiss them, Gubio said without presumption:

"Compose yourself, Saldanha. Now our other two friends are going to wake up.

He caressed Iracema's head and Jorge's poor mother came to herself, exclaiming:

"Where am I?!"

When she saw her husband standing there, she was overcome with emotion, called him by his nickname and shouted:

"Help me! Where is our son? Our son?"

Then, she began speaking as one who has just seen her beloved after a long absence.

Margarida's obsessor was smitten in the innermost fibers of his soul and shed abundant tears. He instinctively looked at Gubio, silently asking him for help.

"What kind of awful dream was that?" asked the unfortunate sister, crying convulsively. "What a filthy place! Have we really crossed over?"

In a fit of desperation, she added:

"I'm afraid the Devil's going to get me! The Devil! O my God! Save me, save me!"

Our Instructor spoke some encouraging words to her and nodded towards her son lying there beside us.

She gradually composed herself and asked Saldanha why he was so quiet, why he wasn't saying those loving and trusting words of days gone by, to which he answered meaningfully:

"Iracema, I still haven't learned how to be useful ... I can't comfort anyone."

At that moment, the reawakened, suffering mother remembered her companion-in-misfortune, who still had her hand around her throat. Barely able to recognize her daughter-in-law, she exclaimed in grief:

"Irene! Irene!"

Gubio intervened with his *awakening* ability and began applying vigorous energies to Irene's cerebral centers.

After a few moments, Saldanha's daughter-in-law stood up with a blood-curdling scream.

She could barely talk. She gurgled loudly, prey to infinite anguish.

Our vigilant guide held both of her hands in his and began applying soothing magnetic resources to her glottis and to her taste buds, especially, thus calming her down somewhat. Although awake, the suicide had not yet fully come to her senses. She did not have the slightest notion of her physical body rotting away in the grave. It was a kind of complete somnambulism, from which she had suddenly woke up.

Finally getting ahold of herself, she approached her husband and exclaimed in a stentorian voice:

"Jorge! Jorge! Thank God the poison didn't kill me after all. Please, forgive my thoughtless deed ... I'll recover and then avenge you! I'll murder the judge that condemned you to such cruel suffering!"

Contrary to what she had expected, her husband did not react, so she implored:

"Listen to me! Where have I been sleeping for so long? Our daughter! Where is she?"

However, Jorge, his perispiritual centers now detached from her direct influence, remained in the same phlegmatic and impassive attitude of someone who was having trouble figuring out his situation.

Gubio approached Irene and explained:

"Compose yourself, my child!"

"Me? Compose myself? No way! I want to go home ... This prison is suffocating me ... Who are you, mister? Please, get me home. My husband has been wrongly imprisoned ... He's obviously out of his mind ... He doesn't listen to me. And my throat is being eaten away by deadly poison ... I want my daughter and a doctor!"

Caressing the girl's brow, our Instructor said in a sad tone:

"Child, when the eyes of your body closed for good, so too did the doors to the home close to your soul. Your husband is free of the commitments of marriage and your daughter has been living in another home for a very long time. You absolutely must redo yourself so that you can help them as much as you want to."

"So, I really am dead? Death is a worse tragedy than life?

"Death is merely a change of dress," Gubio told explained. "We are what we are. After the grave we find nothing but the heaven or hell that we have created for ourselves."

And softening the tone of his voice to speak more like a father, he continued:

"Why did you dispose of the healing medicine by breaking the sacred vile that contained it? Why didn't you ever listen to the chorus of those who were suffering even more than you? Why didn't you ever heed the afflictions that came from deep within you? Why didn't you ever probe the silent suffering of those who had no hands to act, legs to walk, voice to beg?"

"Because rebelliousness consumed me…"

"Yes, one mere moment of rebelliousness puts one's destiny in peril, just as one tiny error in calculation threatens the stability of an entire building."

"O woe is me!" gasped Irene, accepting the bitter reality. "Where was God that he didn't help me in time?"

"Your question is misguided," replied our guide kindly. "Instead, ask yourself if you ever tried to find out what led you to forget God so profoundly. The Lord's goodness never forsakes us. Since you forsook the blessed earthly opportunity that would have led you to spiritual victory, you now must live with the tears of contrition that will lead you to wholesome regeneration. I believe that soon you can attain such a blessing; however, you have carved out a huge precipice between your conscience and the divine harmony you will need to accomplish your recomposition. You will have to live with the consequences of your thoughtless act for quite some time yet. To pick green fruit is to practice violence. You poisoned the delicate matter that makes up the tissues of your soul and few circumstances can mitigate the seriousness of your wrong. However, never give up hope. Press on towards the Good. Even if the horizon at times seems too far away, it is never unreachable."

And encouraging her paternally, he added:

"You'll make it, Irene; you'll make it."

However, amid disappointment and rebelliousness, Irene did not seem interested in grasping such lofty concepts. Diverting her attention from the hard truth, she noticed Saldanha and began to scream.

Gubio sought to calm her down.

Once Jorge's wife overcame her own childish fear, she regressed to her mental intemperance, rested her tormented eyes on her father-in-law and asked:

"Shade or ghost, what are you doing here? Why haven't you avenged your poor son? Doesn't such useless infamy pain you? Have you laid aside the weapons you could use to smite the soulless judge that defiled our lives? Did death make you forsake your devotion to your own parents? Are you going to take it easy in some sort of heaven and watch Jorge reduced to shreds? Or ignore the harsh reality? What compelled you to be silent as a statue? Why haven't you tirelessly sought God's justice, which cannot be found on earth."

Her questions were like blows from a white-hot iron.

Margarida's persecutor received them as an inner beating, because his face was paled with extreme indignation. He wavered, not knowing how to react; but remembering he was in the presence of a wise and loving guide, he looked at Gubio, silently asking for his help. Gubio said in a sad voice:

"Irene, doesn't the certainty of a victorious life beyond death infuse your heart with respect? Do you think we are subject to a power that is unaware of us? Before the new truth that has surprised your soul, can't you perceive the infinite wisdom of a Supreme Giver of all blessings? How can you find happiness in vengeance? The blood and tears of our enemies only deepen the wounds that have opened up in our hearts. Do you think that the true dedication of a father should manifest as dilacerations or murder, persecution or rage? Saldanha came to this prison out of love and I believe that his finest victories have risen, triumphant and renewing, to the surface of his personality! ... Don't cast his fatherly tenderness into the abysm of despair, from whose darkness you have uselessly sought to flee."

The wretched woman fell silent in tears while her father-in-law wiped away those that Gubio's benevolent remarks had elicited from him.

Iracema said that she was exhausted and asked for a cot.

Our guide asked Saldanha to say something.

Although Jorge was feeling better, both discarnate women were in need of immediate help. It would not be right to abandon them to that environment, which could disintegrate the strongest mental energies.

"Certainly," agreed Margarida's greatly-changed obsessor. I know the miscreants around here, and now that Iracema and Irene have come to their senses, I'm concerned about the seriousness of the situation."

Our Instructor said that we would shelter them in a nearby hospital, but we needed his permission.

Saldanha happily acquiesced. Because of our guide's cordial words, he felt stimulated to do what was right, and he showed himself willing to grasp the smallest opportunity to correspond to Gubio's fraternal dedication.

A few minutes later, we left the mental institute with the two women and took them to the hospital, where Gubio got them admitted with all the prestige of his heavenly virtues before the visible amazement of Saldanha, who did not know how to express the gratitude in his soul.

As we were returning, Margarida's persecutor, head-down and humiliated, timidly asked what the right weapons were to use in the work of salvation. Our guide answered attentively.

"In all settings, great love can always assist lesser love to expand its boundaries and impel it towards the higher realms. And everywhere, great, victorious and sublime faith can help small, wavering faith, carrying it to the heights of life."

Saldanha said nothing and we went most of the way back in silence.

13
A Family Get-Together

When we reached the large residence where Margarida was resting, and before approaching her again, Gubio, now assisted a very respectful Saldanha, suggested that we take the opportunity to talk with the judge to determine the situation of Jorge's daughter, who was staying there.

The judge lived with his family in the central wing of the large building where Gabriel and Margarida had their small apartment. Until then, we had not been to that part of the house.

"Maybe," our Instructor said, "we could ask for a meeting of the parties in order to come to an agreement. Surely the judge has a place where we can get together for a few minutes."

Saldanha agreed in monosyllables, like a student who feels obligated to go along with his teacher without arguing.

"The night is propitious," said the Instructor, "and dawn has just begun."

We respectfully went in, but I must say that, due to the large number of suffering spirits who were knocking at the doors of his soul, the judge's sleep was not as peaceful as we would have liked. Some were clamoring for help. Most were demanding justice.

As we were in the judge's private quarters, we saw an incarnate fellow cautiously coming down the stairs.

Saldanha touched Gubio's arm lightly and said:

"That's Alencar, Margarida's brother and my granddaughter's persecutor."

"Let's have a look at him," said the Instructor.

We followed the young man, who was unable to sense our presence. After having gone down a few steps, he stopped at the door to a modest room and tried to force it open.

We could smell his breath and realized that he had been drinking heavily.

"Every night," Saldanha remarked in concern, "he tries to abuse the poor girl. "He doesn't have any self-respect at all. Because Lia resists, he has increased his persecution with various threats, and I think that his unworthy purpose hasn't yet been successful because I'm watching out for her and I defend her with my characteristic brutality."

We were struck by the obsessor's humble tone of voice.

Saldanha seemed viscerally transfigured. His regard for Gubio indicated a sudden transformation. His reverent gestures displayed understanding and tenderness.

Our guide agreed without any airs of superiority:

"In fact, Saldanha, this young man possesses degrading forces and needs energetic assistance that will enable him to seek mental cleanliness."

Gubio began applying magnetic passes over Alencar's eyes.

A few minutes later, Alencar stumbled back to his bedroom with half-closed eyes. Saldanha suggested that some sort of harmless infirmity might encourage him to think about the duties of a moral person for a few days.

Margarida's obsessor displayed undisguised happiness.

We went with our guide back to the judge's private room.

His body was lying on the soft mattress, but his mind was highly troubled.

Gubio urged me to touch the judge's head in order to glean his deepest thoughts.

In that late night hour, the gray-haired gentleman was asking himself: "What is life really all about, after all? Where is the spiritual peace I've been looking for for more than a half century but have never found? Why am I still holding on to the same dreams and needs I had when I was fifteen, when I'm now over sixty?" He had grown up, received an education and gotten married. But all his struggles had not changed him one bit. He had become a "priest of the law" and he had donned the robe hundreds of times to judge complicated cases. He had handed down countless sentences, and by his own designs, he had held the fate of many homes and even whole groups of people in his hands. Due to the position he enjoyed in the decorated ship of the courtroom, he had received the praise of the rich and the poor, the great and the small on his journey across the choppy sea of the earthly experience. He had responded to thousands of cases involving social harmony, but in his inner life a scorching desert filled his entire soul. He longed to be fraternal towards others, but his wealth and his eminence in public life were obstacles that were too big for him to read the truth on their faces. He had an unspeakable hunger for God. Even so, the dogmas and squabbles of the sectarian religions kept his spirit from any accord with faith. On the other hand, negativist, impenitent science had scorched his soul. Could all life actually be summed up as the simple mechanical phenomena of nature? From that point of view, all human life would be about as important as a soap bubble at the mercy of the wind. He felt torn apart, oppressed, exhausted. He, who had enlightened so many regarding the highest standards of personal conduct, how could he enlighten himself at this time in his life? Confronted with the first symptoms of his aging body, he was reacting bitterly against the waning of his organic energies. Why the wrinkles on his face, the graying of his hair, the weakness of his vision and the lessening of his strength if youthfulness still vibrated in his renewal-anxious mind? Was death just a night without a dawn? What mysterious power was leading people's lives towards unexpected and secret objectives?

I removed my hand and saw that the judge had tears in his eyes.

Gubio approached and put his hands on the judge's forehead. He said that he was going to prepare him for our upcoming conversation and that he would help him with his past memories involving Jorge.

After a few moments, the judge's eyes looked different. He seemed to be contemplating far-off scenes of indescribable torment. They were anguishing, full of mental pain...

The Instructor told me to examine his thoughts again and I put my right hand on his brain.

With my general perceptions somewhat developed, I listened to his thoughts once more:

"Why am I thinking about that case?" Margarida's father asked himself. In his opinion, it had been resolved. Why was it troubling him now? Years had passed since that dark crime, but the matter was alive and well in his mind, as if the tyrannical and merciless memory of it was a record involving strange moral suffering. What motives were leading him to remember this case so strongly? In his mind, he saw Jorge, forgotten in the abysm of his subconscious, and remembered his vehement declaration of innocence. He could not explain why he had brought his daughter back to live there. He futilely looked for the secret cause that was making him dwell on the matter on that night of inexplicable insomnia. He remembered Jorge had lost the assistance of his best friends and that his wife had committed suicide in utter despair ... But why was he recalling such an *unimportant* case? He, the judge, called on to decide countless cases, had decided enigmas that were much more intricate and important; thus, he could not explain his memories of that ordinary criminal case involving that plain defendant.

Gubio asked Eloi and me to bring Jorge – now outside his physical body – to the judge's room, while he prepared the judge for a partial detachment from his body by means of sleep.

My companion and I went to the jail cell of the deeply prostrate, obsessed man, who was now outside his body.

I administered reparatory fluids to his perispirit and we took him to the judge's home.

The judge and Saldanha's granddaughter, temporarily liberated from their bodies, were at Gubio's side. He received Jorge with unveiled caring, and bringing the three together, as if he were uniting them in a single, strong magnetic current, he imbued their minds with energies using fluidic procedures so that, awake in spirit, they could hear him as well as possible. I could see that the *awakening* was not the same for all three. It varied according to the evolution and mental state of each of them. The judge was the most lucid due to his sharp mind; the young Lia was next due to the noteworthy qualities of her intelligence; Jorge was last due to his extreme weakness.

When the authoritative exponent of justice found himself in front of the former defendant and his daughter, he asked hesitantly, taken with insufferable shock:

"Where are we? Where are we?"

None of us dared answer.

Gubio was praying silently, however; and when a lovely light radiated from his chest area and head, giving us to understand that sentiment and reason were united in him in celestial clarity, he said to the startled judge while affably patting him on the shoulder:

"A home in the world is not only a shelter for bodies that will change over time. It is also a nest for souls, where spirits can communicate with other spirits when sleep seals the physical lips that are so capable of lying. We have all come together in your home for a hearing with reality."

The head of that domestic sanctuary listened, perplexed.

"The incarnate individual," Gubio continued, "is an immortal soul inhabiting a perishable body, a soul that travels thousands of pathways in order to become one with divine truth, like the pebble that takes centuries to roll down from the top of the mountain to settle in the depths of the sea. Through love and suffering, we are all actors in the sublime drama of universal evolution ... Our interference in the destinies of others is unjust if our feet tread pathways of righteousness. However, if we stray from them, it is right for us to appeal to love so that suffering may diminish."

The magistrate was able to connect these concepts to Jorge's presence, and asked:

"So, are you making an appeal on behalf of this defendant?"

"That's right," responded our Instructor without flinching. "Don't you think that this victim of unconfessable judicial injustice has already drained the cup of suffering?"

"But his case is closed."

"No, not really; none of us has reached the end of our redemptive court cases. Jorge is not the only penitent, convicted wrongdoer worthy of a break from the suffering of remission."

The judge opened his eyes wide, displaying a certain amount of wounded pride, and retorted sarcastically:

"But I was the judge that handled his case. I consulted the statutes before passing sentence. The crime was investigated; the experts' reports and the witnesses condemned the defendant. I cannot in good conscience accept any intromissions, especially this late in the game, without indisputable proof."

Gubio contemplated him compassionately and said:

"I understand your refusal. The fluids of the flesh weave a veil that is too thick to be rent easily by those who do not yet pursue daily contact with the higher realms. You invoke your status as a priest of the law to crush the destiny of a worker who has already lost all he had in order to redeem the wrongs of his distant past. You have referred to the title that human convention bestowed on you, obviously attentive to the injunctions of Divine Power. However, you do not seem to be in conformance with the sublime fundamentals of your lofty mission in the world, because persons who have accepted stewardship in the area of material or spiritual assets while in the world never flaunt their lofty position if they are aware of their responsibilities. They grasp the fact that faithful administration is a pathway of spiritual growth even if it's through extreme moral suffering. To distribute both love and justice on today's earth, on which most people despise such gifts, is to be surrounded by suffering. Do you really believe that people live without being held accountable, even those that believe themselves to be capable of judging their neighbor? Do you really think you have been right regarding all the mysteries along the road? Have you acted impartially in all your decisions? No, you haven't … The Righteous Judge was crucified on a cross because of his devotion to utmost rectitude. All of us on the multi-century road of edifying knowledge too often place desire above duty, and caprice above the redemptive principles we are bound to. On how many occasions have you bent the law to the counterfeit, destructive politics of persons eager for transitory power? In how many cases have you allowed your sentiments to be sullied by personal prejudice?!"

The judge, whom Saldanha regarded as a mortal enemy, was terribly confused. A corpse-like paleness covered his face, on which thick tears began to run. Gubio continued:

"If not for the divine compassion, which, out of love for the Justice you represent, has granted you a number of invisible assistants to help you; if not for the victims of your involuntary errors; and if not for the obsessing passions of those who surround you, you would not have been allowed to remain in your position. Your palatial home is full of darkness. Many of the men and women whom you have sentenced over the more than twenty past years have been taken by death but have not been able to cross over because of the effects of your decisions. They are waiting for you right here in your own home for you to explain yourself. As a missionary of the law, who is not in the habit of prayer and meditation – the only resources by which you can shorten your suffering – you are in for a big surprise when you die."

During a longer pause, the judge displayed indefinable terror in his eyes, fell to his knees and asked:

"I don't know if you are benefactor or avenger, but teach me the way! What can I do for this man I condemned?"

"Review his case and set him free."

"So, he really is innocent?" asked the judge, requiring a solid basis for future conclusions.

"When faced with Heavenly Justice, nobody suffers unnecessarily. The harmony that rules the universe is so great that even our wrongdoings are transubstantiated into blessings. We will explain everything to you."

And showing us that he needed to engrave on the judge's mind everything he would have to do, he continued:

"You will not limit yourself only to freeing Jorge. You are to help your daughter by putting her in a worthy establishment where she can receive the education she needs."

"But this girl isn't my daughter!"

"But you wouldn't be asked to do this if you weren't able to. Do you think that money satisfies only the requirements of those who have joined us according to the ties of blood kinship? Free your soul, my friend! Breathe within a higher atmosphere. Learn to sow love on the ground where you walk. The more eminent our position in the human experience, the more we can work on our spiritual growth. On earth, justice uses courts to try a crime in its varied aspects, thus specializing in determining wrongdoing; however, in heaven, harmony reveals sanctuaries, cherishing our goodness and virtues. They are devoted to upholding the Good in all its divine angles. While there is still time, make Jorge one of your friends and his daughter a companion in the struggle, and someday she will caress your gray hair and offer you the light of prayer when your spirit is compelled to cross over the dark portal of the grave."

"What do I have to do?"

"In the morning you will get out of bed without fully remembering our little conversation, because the corporeal brain is a delicate instrument that cannot bear the load of two lives. Even so, you will have new thoughts that are lovely and clear regarding the good you must do. Intuition is the miraculous tape recorder of the consciousness. It will function freely, retransmitting to you the suggestion of this time of peace and light like a bed of blessings, offering you fragrant and spontaneous flowers. When that happens, do not let reason get in the way of the urge to do good deeds. Within the wavering heart, ordinary reasoning fights against the sentiment of renewal, muddying its clean current with the fear of ingratitude or ruinous obedience to established prejudices."

Before Saldanha, who was watching the scene with ineffable well-being, Jorge and Lia exchanged looks of joy and hope.

The judge looked at them thoughtfully and we could tell that he wanted to ask the Instructor a few more questions. But dominated by the emotions of the moment, he kept still, resigned and humble.

Gubio, however, scanned the man's thoughts, touched his forehead lightly and said in a firm voice:

"You would like me to tell you whether Jorge is really innocent so that your conscience as a judge can consolidate certain points of view regarding his case. Yes, as far as the crime is concerned, Jorge's hands are clean. Nonetheless, a human life is like a priceless fabric that mortal eyes can only see one side of. In the sufferings of today, we pay the debts of yesterday. We do not mean that our wrongs, which are usually caused by the idleness or impenitence of today, causing harmful results for ourselves and others, are providential resources for paying old debts, because then we would be consecrating fatalism as ruler of the world, whereas at every moment, we are creating causes and effects with our daily actions. The entities that weep at your gates are there for a reason, and sooner or later, the robe you are wearing for now will have to make amends with all those who lament around it. But Jorge, who didn't come here to complain, but to take part in beneficial understanding, has rid himself of a certain part of the dolorous past."

Gubio paused, looked deeply at the judge and continued gravely:

"Persons and successes that may affect the conscience in a particular way are not an ordinary object on the revealing march of life. For now, your mind is subject to the biological shock of the return to the flesh and you could not follow us in the exhumation of the recent past. Nevertheless, I have examined your mental archives and have seen scenes that time cannot destroy. During the last century, you owned a large amount of land and you prided yourself for your position as master of dozens of slaves. Most of them have reincarnated and make up your group of legal assistants. You owe assistance and care, help and understanding to all of them. However, not all your former slaves fall into the same group with regards to your spirit. Some have stood out in your life drama and are back on your path to make a special impact on you. Jorge, for instance, was one of your slaves, although he was born under the same roof that marked your first cries at birth. He may have been your slave according to earthly codes, but he was your brother according to the divine laws, in spite of having been born of a different mother. You never forgave him for such closeness, considered in your home as an insult to the family name. You both became fathers and your son of then and now sexually abused his daughter of then and now, and faced with such bitterness, with utmost scorn for a slave's sad home, you took condemnable measures that culminated in unspeakable despair for the Jorge of back then, who, aimless and half-crazy, not only took the life of your son, who had invaded his home, but also his own life by committing suicide under dramatic circumstances. However, neither death nor suffering can erase the afflictions of responsibility, which only a renewed opportunity for reconciliation can remedy. Now here you are, once again in the presence of Jorge, whom you have hated needlessly, and the young woman, whom you promised to look after as your dearest daughter. Work, my friend! Take advantage of the years left to you because Alencar and your ward will be attracted to the blessings of marriage. Work while you still can. All the good that you do will work on your own behalf, for there is no other pathway to God other than constructive understanding, active goodness and redemptive forgiveness. Jorge, humiliated and disillusioned, has erased his deplorable wrong by having to endure unspeakable moral suffering during a few years of undeserved condemnation and torturous imprisonment, with widowhood, infirmities and privations of all sorts."

Our instructor paused to look mercifully into the judge's eyes and asked:

"Are you ready to make amends?"

Hidden to us, a wholesome jolt had an obvious impact on the spirit of the judge, whose face was completely transformed. He stood up in tears and staggered around. The Instructor's magnetic energies had touched his innermost fibers, for his eyes seemed illumined with sudden determination.

He approached Jorge, held out his hand as a sign of fraternity – which Saldanha's son kissed in tears – and then went over to the young woman, opened his arms to her and exclaimed:

"You shall be my daughter from now on!"

That unforgettable moment made us indescribably happy.

Gubio helped them back to their rooms, and when we took Jorge to the hospital where his resting body awaited him, Saldanha, completely changed by a mysterious joy reflected in his facial expressions, approached our Instructor, and trying to kiss his hands, he said:

"I never thought I would have a night as glorious as this one!"

Saldanha was about to go into a long acknowledgement, but Gubio told him to compose himself, adding:

"Saldanha, apart from God's love, there is no joy as great as the kind we find in the spontaneous love of a friend. Such joy is ours at this moment because we feel your noble and sincere friendship within our hearts."

An embrace of loving fraternity crowned the touching and unforgettable scene.

14
An Extraordinary Event

When we entered the room where Margarida was resting, we found the two hypnotizers hard at work.

Gubio gave Saldanha a meaningful look and said to him discreetly:

"My friend, it's my turn to ask you to do something for me. Please forgive me for having taken so long to reveal who I really am and what my objectives are."

And with great emotion in his voice, he explained:

"Saldanha, this sick woman has been the daughter of my soul for ages. I feel the same love for her that you have had for Jorge, defending him with all your might. I know that the struggle has pierced your heart with sharp barbs, but I too have the sentiments of a father. Don't I deserve sympathy and help too? We are brothers in our devotion to our children and we are comrades in the same struggle."

I then observed a touching scene that just minutes before would have seemed unbelievable.

Margarida's persecutor contemplated our Instructor with the look of a repentant son. Thick tears burst forth from his formerly cold and impassive eyes. He seemed unable to respond due to the emotion that had overcome his throat; however, Gubio embraced him fraternally and added:

"We have just had a sublime time of endeavor, understanding and forgiveness. Wouldn't you like to forgive those who hurt you and thus liberate the one who is so dear to my heart? There always comes a time when we finally grow weary of our wrongful ways. Our soul is bathed in the lustral fount of regenerative tears and we forget all evil to embrace all the good. In times gone by, I too persecuted and humiliated others. I didn't believe in any good deeds that I myself didn't do. I thought I was noble and invincible, whereas I was merely wretched and insensitive. I regarded those who didn't understand my perilous whims or praise my insanity as enemies. It was diabolically pleasurable for me when an enemy would beg for my prideful mercy, and I loved to practice humiliating benevolence towards those beneath me. But life, which breaks down stone with drops of water, shredded my heart with the dagger of time, slowly transforming me so that the despot within me finally died. Now, being called a brother is the only thing I am really proud of. Saldanha, my friend, tell me that hatred has also died in your spirit; tell me I can count on your blessed assistance!"

Eloi and I shed ardent tears as a result of that emotional and unexpected lesson.

Saldanha wiped his eyes and humbly said to Gubio:

"Nobody has ever spoken to me as you have ... Your words are consecrated by a divine power that I cannot grasp, because they reach my ears while I am still puzzled by your convincing actions. Do with me what you will. This very night you have adopted as children of your heart all my family members who still remember me. You have assisted my demented son; you have reoriented my insane wife; you have seen to my unfortunate daughter-in-law; you have helped my defenseless granddaughter, and you have rebuked those who trouble me unfairly ... How could I not join hands with you to help save the poor woman whom you love as a daughter? Even if she were to stab me a thousand times, what you have done for me would redeem her in my eyes."

And trying to hold back his tears, the ex-persecutor said reverently:

"Powerful spirit and good friend, you came to me as a servant to awaken my energies frozen in the ice of revenge. I am ready and willing to serve you! I am yours from here on out!"

"We are Jesus' own forever!" corrected Gubio.

And embracing Saldanha effusively, Gubio led him into the adjoining room to draw up an effective and efficient plan of action.

Only then did I remember the two hypnotizers working industriously on the couple. One of them seemed troubled and obviously aware that something extraordinary was happening, but perhaps compelled by vows of discipline, he did not say anything to us. The other one displayed no emotion whatsoever. He continued, oblivious to what was going on. He looked like an automaton and I was particularly struck by his impassive look.

A few onerous minutes passed, when Gubio and Saldanha came back.

Margarida's former obsessor seemed changed, almost powerless. He was at the gates of inner renewal.

Evidently, while he was with our guide, he had drawn up a new plan, because he called the most active hypnotizer to have a private talk.

The conversation unfolded clearly next to me.

"Leoncio," said Saldanha enthusiastically, "our plans have changed and your help is needed."

"Oh? What happened?"

"Something extraordinary!"

And he continued, transformed:

"There is a wizard of the divine light here."

Saldanha quickly outlined what had happened that night and ended by appealing: "So, can we count on you?"

"But of course! Your friends are my friends, in spite of the risks of the undertaking."

And nodding toward the other magnetizer, who was continuing his work on Margarida like a machine, he warned:

"We have to be really cautious about Gaspar. I don't think he'll be able to go along with it."

"Don't worry," said Saldanha. "We'll handle it."

Leoncio's eyes shone and he said to his ex-boss in a pleading voice:

"Listen! You're aware of my problem. If that wizard helped you, do you think he would do the same for me? My wife is being seduced and my son is dying."

And in a more forceful tone, he added:

"Saldanha, you know I'm a criminal, but I'm a father too ... If I could save my son from rebelliousness and death while there's still time, I would be extremely grateful. You know that a criminal doesn't want his children to follow in his footsteps!"

Saldanha did not hesitate before that tearful appeal:

"OK, then. Go ahead and explain your case to the benefactor Gubio."

Leoncio did not hesitate.

He respectfully approached our Instructor and explained himself simply and shamelessly:

"My friend, I just found out how eagerly you use your powers for folks who have strayed from the Good; for folks like us, for instance, who feel despicable before everyone. That's why I, too, am begging you for your immediate help."

"What can we do for you?"

"I came here seven long years ago, leaving my wife and a new-born son behind. I was still young when I died of exhaustion from working too hard in search of easy money. And I did accomplish my aim, which was to have a nice, healthy bank account. As a result, my wife has been well provided for. But the desperation and useless anxiety at trying to return to the body I had abandoned, in addition to my wounded pride, turned me into the inhuman collaborator that our boss Gregorio is so proud of ... Woe is me! I saw myself as the exclusive owner of my beloved wife's affections! Two years ago, my poor Avelina began to heed the outrageous proposals of a male nurse who took advantage of my son's poor health to get to her, a widowed young mother. He had been called to help the boy after an unimportant incident and noticed his prey's material possessions. He began to pursue my wife relentlessly, and according to his cruel plans, he began to poison my son bit by bit with narcotics. He finally got what he wanted from Avelina: money, illusions, pleasures and a promise of marriage. I think they are going to get married in a few days and I've resigned myself to it, because the incarnate soul lives in a thick web of nightmares and demands. But the disguised persecutor sees my son as a competitor for the assets I accumulated. He wants to get him out of the way as soon as possible and rob him of his right to a worthy and happy future."

He paused for a few moments and then continued emotionally:

"To be honest, I'm ashamed to ask for a favor that I don't deserve. But perverted spirit that I know I am, I'm asking for your help to save my loved ones, in spite of the evil I have chosen to inspire my pathway ... Benefactor, have mercy! My poor Angelo is at the brink of the grave ... I think he's going to be dead in just a few days if kindly, devoted hands don't help us in our helplessness. I've done all I can, but I'm an integral member of a phalanx of evil spirits, and evil can't save or help anyone."

Gubio was about to respond, but Eloi interrupted. To our great surprise, he asked unceremoniously:

"What's this male nurse's name? Who is this child killer?"

"Felicio de ..."

When he heard the family name, Eloi grabbed ahold of me to keep from falling over:

"That's my brother!" he cried, "my brother!"

His face was pale with emotion. Anguished expectation fell over us.

But Gubio embraced Eloi and asked with the supreme serenity that was part of his character:

"Eloi, show me just one person who is not a brother or sister in need."

That intelligent and kindly statement quieted our smitten colleague down.

Perhaps desiring to dispel the clouds that had darkened the place and to transform it into a blessed sanctuary, our Instructor invited us to leave right away to pay the dying boy a visit.

Saldanha nodded toward the odd figure of Gaspar, who seemed deaf and insensitive to what was going on, and remarked:

"Let's leave him alone for a few hours. Besides, we need at least one day to fortify our defenses. Gregorio's phalanx is not going to forgive us."

Our Instructor smiled without saying anything and we left.

A fresh, cool morning breeze was blowing but a restless quietude reigned over the suburban streets as we quickly made our way.

Leoncio led the way, finally showing us a comfortable-looking home and saying:

"This is the place."

We went in.

The mother and the nurse were sleeping alone in separate rooms, while a little boy was crying almost imperceptibly in his, displaying anguish and malaise.

I could see the devastation done to him by the toxins. His eyes displayed profound sadness.

Leoncio, the fearsome hypnotizer, embraced him and explained:

"The subtle poisons that he has been ingesting in small, systematic doses have permeated his body and soul."

I could tell that invisible, magnetic threads connected father and son, because, in spite of his dreadful condition, the boy, with a look of rapture, contemplated the large portrait of his father hanging on the wall and asked in a weak voice:

"Daddy, where are you? … I'm scared; really scared."

Ardent tears followed this unexpected appeal and Margarida's hypnotizer, who had until then seemed like a dreadful entity, broke down and wept.

Gubio left for a few moments and returned with Felicio, the nurse, who was temporarily outside his body. Despite being semi-conscious, when the young man saw Eloi beside the sick boy, he tried to withdraw in an impulse of obvious fear. However, Gubio gently prevented it.

Eloi's physiognomy had changed as he approached Felicio to have a word with him.

Our Instructor patted him with his right hand and warned:

"Don't interfere, Eloi. You're in no emotional condition to assist effectively. Your anger would render you useless for this type of work. We'll need you later on."

Gubio began applying magnetic passes of *awakening* to Felicio so that his mind could grasp the lesson in the highest state of consciousness possible. The subject began to gaze at us more clearly, although ashamed and skittish. He was positively terrified when he saw Eloi, and when he saw Leoncio weeping over his son, he tried once more to get away. Then he asked:

"What's this? That monster's actually shedding some tears?"

Gubio used that brutally sarcastic question to start his intervention:

"Don't you think a father has the right to be distraught over his persecuted, sick son?"

"I just know that he's my bloodthirsty enemy," said Eloi's brother with insufferable animosity. I recognized him right away. He's Avelina's husband ... At first, I only saw the pictures of him here ... but then he began to hound me as I slept."

"Listen!" said Gubio kindly. "Who assumed the status of enemy in the first place: Leoncio, who was humiliated and hurt in his innermost sentiments, or you, with your deplorable plan to win over a defenseless widow? Leoncio, who suffers as a devoted father, or you, with your sinister plan to murder his son?"

"But Leoncio's dead!"

"And won't you be dead someday too? Won't your own body of flesh return to dust someday?"

And because Felicio could not respond due to being overwhelmed by guilt, the Instructor continued:

"Felicio, why do you insist on going through with this coldhearted crime? Don't you have any pity at all for a sick child who has no visible father? You call Leoncio a monster for defending the frail lamb of his heart, like a powerless bird that attacks in order to defend its nest ... Well, what about you, my brother? Didn't your instinct for pleasure and power lead you to invade this sanctuary? What about your regrettable actions as a nurse, who has been using his divine gift to soothe and heal to trouble and wound instead? Felicio, compared with the eternity in which consciousness moves, the human experience is a mere dream or nightmare only a few minutes long. Why are you compromising your future at the cost of the illusory comfort of only a few days? Those who sow thorns will reap thorns in their own soul and will appear before the Lord with hands changed into abominable claws. Those who scatter stones around the feet of others will be overcome by the hardness and paralysis of their own heart. Do you have any idea of the responsibility you are assuming? In your heart there are still obvious vestiges of the goodness of a blessed and great family where solidarity is cultivated from the very start of the struggle. I can see that youthful enthusiasm has not vanished completely from your mind. So, why give in to the suggestions of crime? Doesn't the prostration of this child you're inflicting with a slow death move you? Listen to me! Leoncio's situation doesn't boil down to the conflict of a so-called 'dead' man, as you might suppose in your disturbed mind. His heart is that of a loving, devoted father! You will find that he is full of gentle, pure love, just like the hidden gleam in a rough, unpolished gem."

Eloi's brother looked at our Instructor with fearful, wondrous eyes.

After a short pause, Gubio continued:

"Come here. Come to us. Have you lost your ability to love? Leoncio is your friend and our brother."

Felicio cried out with a visible expression of anguish:

"I want to be good but I can't ... I've tried to better myself but just can't ..."

In a tear-choked voice he added:

"What about the money? How am I going to pay off all those debts unless I marry Avelina?!"

"And you think you can solve your money problems by piling up moral debts that will torment you for a long, long time? Nobody's stopping you from marrying; not even Leoncio, the one whose assets you plan to spend capriciously, can keep you from it. Each man's and each woman's actions structure their destinies. We are responsible for all our decisions in light of the designs of the Eternal One and we cannot interfere with your free will. Even so, we are asking for your help on behalf of this fragile life that must continue living ... You want money, assets that will make you respected or feared by others. But you have to remember that wealth is a crown that is too heavy for the head of the one who cannot handle it, and through exhaustion and disillusionment, it usually ruins all those who would have it without the broad horizons of work and charity. So it doesn't matter if you control the priceless deposits of silver and gold that Leoncio amassed inadvertently, because with time you will learn that happiness is not measured by the coffers that rust will consume someday. On the other hand, Felicio, we are interested in your promise on behalf of this poor suffering child. Spare his tender body and wait for the future! Do not carry such a crime into the kingdom of death. It would condemn your spirit to the dreadful caves of regenerative expiation."

Felicio wanted to say something to justify himself but couldn't.

Gubio continued serenely:

"Go ahead and marry. Squander the precious reserves of this home if you can't grasp the sacred purpose of money in time. Soar to the heights of transitory societal life. Decorate yourself with the conventional titles that the lower world is accustomed to awarding to sagacious individuals who climb the ladder of futile or ruinous domination without publically wounding their prejudices. But time will be waiting for you with masterful lessons. I would urge you, however, to help the little one to recover his health."

And looking compassionately at Margarida's hypnotizer, he asked:

"Isn't that what we all want, after all, Leoncio?"

"Oh, yes!" confirmed the poor father in loving tears. "I don't care about the money and I can now see that Avelina is as free as I am. But if my little one is to remain on earth, I am hopeful about my own regeneration. He will be my companion and friend, connected to my memory, in whose capacity to serve I will find a blessed arena of spiritual work. Meanwhile, this child is the only means I have to believe once again in the good that I have avoided."

Recognizing how hard it was for him to speak, Gubio embraced him, stood him on his feet and said:

"Leoncio, Jesus believes in people's cooperation, just as he puts up with our stubborn imperfections until we accept the imperative of our personal conversion to the ultimate Good. So why have we disbelieved? I believe in Felicio's renewal. From this day forward, your little one will no longer be watched over by a persecutor but by a benefactor worthy of our fraternal concourse!"

Won over by such words, Felicio knelt down before us and swore:

"In the name of Divine Justice, I promise to protect this child as a true father!"

He stood up and tried to kiss Gubio's hands, but our Instructor politely refused the homage and asked Eloi and me to take the patient back to his physical body while he himself would apply strengthening passes to the child.

Felicio held on to us, and after we helped him back into his body, he woke up in copious tears.

Things did not end there, however.

Forcing the situation somewhat, Eloi applied a strong magnetic current over his brother's eyes. Still groggy, Felicio saw the two of us for a few seconds.

Mouth agape, he did not know what to say. But with righteous indignation, Eloi warned him frankly:

"If you murder that boy, I will punish you myself!"

Felicio let out a dreadful scream and fainted on his pillow, losing us from view.

I knew then and there that Felicio would fulfill his promise to the letter.

15
Help at Last

Enthusiastic about what our Instructor was doing, Saldanha displayed gestures of almost child-like humility, and both he and Leoncio began to cooperate with us in our preparations to bring the case to an end.

Both suggested that they be allowed to stay there with us so that we would not unwittingly awaken the fury of the ignorant spirits who would be against our purposes. They might organize themselves into a threatening legion and ruin our plans. The pair knew procedures of assistance like the one we were using and they were well-informed about the potential of the enemy region, from which hundreds of adversaries could instantly rise up against that home, which was ill-prepared to resist such an attack.

As I listened to their opinions, I was concerned about Gaspar and could not hide my misgivings about him. The hypnotizer, displaying a highly disagreeable presence due to the fluids he was emitting, was not taking part in our discussion. His semi-glazed eyes could not focus on us, suggesting a sort of soul paralysis or thought petrification.

I was unable to contain my curiosity any longer, so I asked Gubio about Gaspar's situation. What was the meaning of that psychological mask he was wearing? He seemed deaf, almost blind, and completely unfeeling. He answered long, important questions with vague, monosyllables, and he displayed an unbending insistence on punishing his victim.

The Instructor was now free of concerns and explained:

"Andre, there are many obsessors who are markedly hard of heart when under the influence of persecutors that are even stronger and more wicked than they. These fearsome intelligences of the darkness control specific perispiritual centers of certain spirits who are wicked and ungrateful towards the Good. They use them as instruments to extend the evil they have chosen to sow. Gaspar is in that situation. Hypnotized by lords of disorder and anesthetized by numbing rays, he has temporarily lost his ability to see, hear and feel clearly. He is held in a troubling nightmare in which Margarida's suffering is his single obsession."

"Won't he ever be able to regain his natural senses?" I asked in amazement.

"Of course he will. Magnetism is a universal force that follows the direction we give it. Applying passes to neutralize the paralysis will restore him to normality. Such an operation, however, has to be done at the right time. Intensive regenerative resources are necessary, resources that are most likely to be found in groups where several collaborating individuals are in tune with one another on behalf of just one, if need be."

Just then, Saldanha approached trustingly to ask for instructions.

"My Benefactor," Saldanha addressed Gubio reverently, "revealing the new situation too soon could cause an awful reaction against our efforts by the wrong persons. Quite frankly, this is all new to me and I don't know where to start."

"Yes, I'm afraid you're right about that, Saldanha. We are too weak to fight against so many. It is absolutely essential that Margarida recover somewhat before we do anything more. Let's wait for nightfall. I intend to take the case to a group focused on fraternal love. Until then, we need to keep things as they are; besides, Gaspar is also in need of special attention. His perispirit is very sick and corrupted and in need of charitable assistance."

Gubio had barely finished his remarks, when Gabriel entered the room and sat next to his dispirited and smitten wife.

Now in charge of the situation, Gubio approached him gently and placed his fatherly right hand on Gabriel's brow to instill his mind with inspiration by giving course to the magnetic forces capable of arriving at a favorable solution to the case.

I noticed that, under this renewing influence, Margarida's husband began to lovingly contemplate his wife. He held her hands with real tenderness and said:

"Margarida, it pains me to see you like this, so downcast."

Neither one said anything for a while, until Gabriel, with a light of indefinable hope in his eyes, exclaimed:

"Listen! I just got an idea. It's been several days now and all these strong medicines and drastic measures haven't done a thing for you. Would you be willing to let me seek the help of a friend of mine who is involved in Christian Spiritism?"

Touched by that wave of blessed caring, which flowing imperceptibly from Gubio through Gabriel, the patient opened her eyes, full of renewed interest, as if she had found an unexpected pathway to salvation. She agreed happily:

"I'm ready and willing. I'll agree to any means that you might consider as right and worthy."

In a rapture of hope, Gabriel left in a hurry, followed by Gubio, who asked us to stay behind with Saldanha and get ready for that night's work.

I did not waste any time in getting to know the ex-persecutor better.

This experience was completely new to me and I wanted to broaden my knowledge and resources. I thought of myself as an incomplete worker; thus I needed to keep on learning. I approached the tormenter-turned-friend and asked:

"Saldanha, I was wondering why we have to be so concerned about our wayward fellow spirits."

He looked at me in amazement and replied:

"My dear friend, I have a full grasp of the situation. If we were to fight openly with this young woman at our side while she is so weak physically, we would suffer defeat in a matter of minutes. Here, in these lower realms, evil is the dominant force everywhere. We are being watched closely and we can't do a thing about it. To confront the evil and defeat it, we have to have the prudence and selflessness of the angels; otherwise, we are wasting our time and we would fall, defenseless, into the perilous traps of the darkness."

Our new ally glanced around the room to check whether or not we were being listened to by enemies, and then continued:

"Take me, for instance. Right after I got here I did everything I could to run from evil – but it was futile. Time had not wiped from my memory the old prayers I had learned at home, but when I said them out loud they only aroused the cruel sarcasm of the enemies of the Good. Even though the will to improve myself was sincere in my heart, the truth of the matter was that my head was full of bad thoughts. I made some effort to resist, but down deep, my impulse towards the true Good was a mild breeze before a typhoon. Surrounded by all these wretched, vengeful discarnates, I lost what moral composure I still had left. If the soul, freed from the corporeal body, is not endowed with strong principles of sanctifying virtue, it is nearly impossible to come out victorious from the dark traps they set for us."

"But," I objected, "isn't that attitude merely a reflection of unsustainable ignorance?"

"I guess so," Saldanha conceded, surprising me with the clarity of his argumentation; "however, you know that the greatest difficulty is not due to our ignorance per se, but our hardheartedness against change. Wisdom overcomes ignorance; goodness humiliates perversity; and true love surrounds hatred in an iron circle; even so, those that are willingly stranded in the lower regions wield a thousand weapons of spite, slander, envy, jealousy, lies and discord against the Good, causing mental imbalance and discouragement."

As I thought about the resourceful, clear logic of what he was saying, I stated:

"Your own case is a living example. I'm surprised by your intelligent remarks. There's no way you can be seen as ignorant."

"Oh, I'm intelligent, all right," replied the ex-tormenter with a smile. "Educated, too. I'm fully informed about all my duties. Even so, I need the company of someone who can show me the effectiveness and security of the Good amid so much evil.   Let's imagine someone who's hungry, listening to a lecture. Do you think words are going to satisfy the demands of his stomach? Well, that's exactly what happened in my case. I was so preoccupied with my wife and daughter-in-law that had discarnated in such dreadful mental imbalance, and I was so tormented by my crazy son and granddaughter, that there was no 'mental room' in my head for theories about salvation. The kindly Gubio, however, has shown me that good is more powerful than evil. That was quite enough to satisfy me.

During times of doubt, beneficial enlightenment characterizes true charity."

Saldanha looked around with a look of extreme distrust and emphasized:

"However, from my own experience I do know who the rebellious spirits are, because they comprise a group that I was part of until just yesterday. To be honest, I'm not really sure what's going to happen to me. They'll probably hound me without mercy. If they can, they'll haul me off to the valley of unspeakable misery. Even so, I can foresee my spirit's wholesome transformation. I'm sure that good can overcome evil and I hope that our Instructor will not forsake me. Even if I do have to suffer, I will follow him. I don't plan on going back to my former, repugnant ways."

Leoncio, who had been following our conversation, stated in turn:

"I can't serve in the ranks of vengeance any longer either. I've had enough of it…"

I told them that I understood, and on behalf of our guide, I promised they could count on shelter on a higher plane.

They were smiling happily when Gubio returned to the patient's quarters and informed us that the problem had been taken care of. That night, Margarida and Gabriel would be attending a family meeting, an important center of mediumistic help.

The incarnate patient and her traumatized hypnotizer would both receive effective resources.

We eagerly waited for nightfall.

From time to time, Gubio would place his hand on the patient's brow to increase her overall resistance.

Around 8:00 p.m., a car arrived to pick up the couple. They were accompanied by us and the large group of "ovoids" that were still connected to the patient's brain through *magnetization.*

Saldanha had taken measures to outwit all the trouble-making spirits who had planned on following us. He had put them at ease, saying that the matter was being taken care of, which was a fact.

When we arrived at the comfortable abode, we were well-received.

Mr. Silva, the head of the family, welcomed Gabriel and Margarida with unequivocal displays of caring. Sidonio, the spirit director of the upcoming work, extended his fraternal arms to us.

Inside were four men and three women, the usual members of the family circle. They began exchanging thoughts with the visitors, reassuring them and explaining what would be happening. Finally, the clock showed that it was time to get started.

Gubio asked about the group, and Sidonio explained:

"Our group has been having satisfactory results; nonetheless, it could do an even better job if the trust in the Good and the ideal of serving were stronger amongst our collaborators in the physical realm. We know that the instrumentality is an essential part of any type of endeavor. The arm is the instrument of the thought; the worker is the supplement of the administrator; the apprentice is the vehicle of the master. If we do not have any incarnates to correspond to our sanctifying objectives, how can higher spirituality be established on the earth? In fact, we have found brothers and sisters who are ready and willing to lend their fraternal concourse, but needless to say, most of them are hoping for some sort of spectacular display of mediumship to warrant cooperating with us. They don't seem to realize that all of us are mediums of either good or evil to some degree, depending on our receptive faculties. They do not accept the requirements of the service that urge us to seek self-enlightenment by serving our fellow beings, and they expect mediumistic gifts, as if they were miraculous bestowals to be given gladly to those who want their benefits using the old 'magic wand.' They seem to have forgotten that mediumship is an energy that everyone possesses to a greater or lesser extent of exteriorization, an energy that is subject to the principles of direction and the law of use, just like a hoe can be used to either serve or harm, depending on the impulse that directs it. Mediumship continues to strengthen when used methodically, whereas it gets covered with asphyxiating and destructive rust if it is left lying around. Our friends do not realize the value of a fearless attitude and positive faith on the praiseworthy pathway, come what may. And although we look after their faith with the same care that an industrious farmer looks after the tender shoot that contains the hope of the future, all it takes is a subtle visit by malicious and perverse spirits, like blackbirds in a rice field, and the fine seeds that we have incessantly planted in the soil of their hearts fail to sprout. From one moment to the next, they doubt our efforts, they distrust themselves, and they close their eyes to the grandeur of the laws that surround them in the nooks and crannies of nature. The mental energies that they should use to focus on active and sanctifying construction with an eye on their own spiritual growth are discarded almost daily by the deceitful arguments of ungrateful and ignorant spirits."

Taking advantage of a pause, I ventured to ask:

"Can that be the case in a group that is as harmoniously constituted as this one? Are we to believe that a group that has been organized for wholesome purposes like this one can become a den of depressing forces?"

Sidonio smiled good-humoredly and replied:

"Yes, considered collectively, they are all together right now under this friendly roof and are seeking our spiritualizing company. But that is for only six out of the 168 hours of the week. While here with us, they are enveloped in gentle radiations of peace and joy, of good cheer and hope as they register our edifying vibrations, of which we'd love for them to be sure and permanent bearers, taking them into the daily realm of the human struggle. However, as soon as they are only a little ways from these doors, they accept or send out thousands of subtle thoughts that are much different from the ones we had suggested to them; thoughts that conflict with our work plan; thoughts, which, born from the minds of incarnates and discarnates, flog us mercilessly. Very few understand that faith is a blessing that can be increased indefinitely. Hence, they flee the work that the preservation, consolidation and growth that such a gift offers to all of us. Furthermore, when this or that brother or sister displays an advanced ability to serve the common good on behalf of the realm of light during sleep, they are usually, visited immediately by bad spirits that are interested in extending the realm of darkness. They break down their convictions and newly-born purposes with unwholesome insinuations if their minds are not supported appropriately by an intense desire to progress, redeem themselves and press forward."

This explanation was highly interesting and it would have been nice to have heard more on the subject, but the clock showed that it was time for us to get to work.

For the endeavors of the meeting, consisting of nine incarnates, there were twenty-one spirit collaborators from our plane of action.

Gubio and Sidonio worked together giving Margarida magnetic passes to finally detach the "ovoid bodies," which were then entrusted to a commission of six fellow spirits, who, in turn, carefully took them to emergency outposts.

Then, during the prayer and the gospel study amid contributions from our sphere, a large amount of neural energy, with just the right amount of reinvigorating fluids from our plane, was extracted from the mouths, nostrils and hands of the incarnate assistants. Sidonio and Gubio then applied these energies to Margarida and Gaspar to restore their own perispiritual energies.

Margarida immediately began to display blessed signs of relief, and Gaspar, impassive as he had been, began to moan, as if he were waking up from a long, frightful nightmare.

At this point, Gubio prepared Dona[15] Isaura – the lady of the house and medium for the meeting – by applying magnetic passes to her larynx and especially to her nervous system, thus assisting her faculty of incorporation.[16] When the time came for the incarnates to begin their work of Christian love on behalf of the discarnates, the guides led Gaspar over to the medium so that he could receive some benefit upon coming in contact with the incarnates, who began supplying him with vitalizing energies, as happens to flowers that support the wholesome toil of industrious bees without even realizing it.

I could see that the senses of the unfeeling persecutor took on an unexpected perception. His vision, hearing, touch and smell suddenly woke up and intensified. He seemed like an awakening somnambulist. The more he combined his own energies with those of the medium, the more his senses were reactivated. As he temporarily grasped Dona Isaura's organic resources by means of "psychic grafting," the hypnotizer cried out and began weeping

---

15 In Brazilian society, *Dona* is a term of respect that is used with the woman's first name. – Tr.

16 Also called 'Psychophony' – communication by spirits through the voice of a speaking medium. This takes place from 'perispirit' to 'perispirit' since the discarnate does not 'enter' the medium's body. See *The Mediums' Book,* by Allan Kardec (International Spiritist Council), and *Missionaries of the Light,* chapter 16 'Incorporation,' by the spirit Andre Luiz, psychographed by Francisco Candido Xavier (International Spiritist Council). – Tr.

ruefully. He mixed blasphemies with tears and moving words with bad ones amid penitence and rebelliousness. With his hearing now fully restored, he could converse clearly with the meeting's instructor. In a spiritually constructive lesson that touched our innermost fibers, Mr. Silva, Isaura's husband, enabled Gaspar to grasp the need for spiritual renewal. After a full hour of exhaustive emotional dialogue, two assistants from our team took him to a place for mentally imbalanced spirits, where he could gradually recover his right mind.

When the work was finished, the meeting ended and an immense joy overflowed from everyone's hearts.

Margarida felt relief at last. In tears she asked Gabriel to thank everybody for the gift she had received.

Gubio, however, saw that Saldanha was a bit unnerved and remarked:

"This is not yet the final triumph. Margarida has received immediate assistance, but we must now assist her home until she can fully incorporate the benefits she has received into her individuality."

He smiled benevolently and added:

"For a plant to be useful, it is not enough for it to be beautiful and fragrant in a protective greenhouse. It needs to be outside, where it can consolidate its strength in order to be utilized for the common good."

Arriving at an understanding with Sidonio, Gubio elicited the collaboration of twelve assistants for ten days to reinforce the defensive activities at Gabriel's home, since, according to Saldanha and Leoncio, starting tomorrow we could expect all-out war with Gregorio's henchmen, who would descend on us, dreadful and persistent.

16
Pernicious Witchery

When the meeting ended, I noticed that the medium, Dona Isaura Silva, had undergone a perceptible transfiguration.

While we were working, she had displayed shiny radiations around her brain, offering a pleasant personal ambient; however, by the time the session was over, she was surrounded by a dark gray fluidic substance, as if around her an invisible light had suddenly been switched off.

Astonished, I approached Sidonio, who kindly responded:

"The poor thing is caught up in a veritable tempest of malignant fluids sent by low order spirits, whom she has inadvertently tuned in to through the dark wires of jealousy. As long as she is under our direct influence, particularly during spiritual endeavors of a collective nature, in which she acts as a receiving valve for the assistants' energies, she is happy and in a good mood. A medium is always a source that both gives and receives during his or her work involving the two realms. When Isaura's work ends, however, she falls back into her unfortunate condition."

"But isn't there anything we can do to help?"

"Of course, and it is because we haven't forsaken her that she has not yet succumbed. Even so, in a case like this we have to be careful not to humiliate or hurt her. When we are taking care of a young shoot, from which we hope to pick a flower someday, we have to fight off invasive insects without hurting it. To parch the sprout of today is to lose the harvest of tomorrow. Our sister is a precious coworker with appreciable and invaluable qualities, but she has not yet let go of her jealousy regarding her husband. It is through that breach that violent vibrations of anger get in, causing her to lose excellent opportunities to serve and grow spiritually. Today she had one of her worst days, completely handing herself over to such inner flagellation. She needs our help tonight because whenever a servant, awakened to the good, endures a wave of inferior vibrations throughout the day, he or she is setting up a visit with the beings and forces that populate the night."

He had a meaningful expression on his face and added:

"As long as persons have no real aspirations of a higher nature, evil intelligences don't even bother with them; but as soon as they display purposes of sublimation and begin to purify their vibrational tone, their spiritual growth starts to be noticed and they are persecuted by spirits who delight in jealousy or rebelliousness."

I could see that Isaura's case could be highly important for my particular studies. Realizing that Margarida had already been helped a great deal, I asked our Instructor, with Sidonio's consent, if I could stay behind to study the troubling conflict between the missionary and those who would influence the dark screen of her sentiments that night.

Gubio agreed with a smile.

He would wait for my return the following day.

My group left, taking the infinitely happy patient and husband with them. I engaged in a conversation with Sidonio.

"For the time being," he explained, "this house is under our watch-care. Even though trouble-making or criminal spirits cannot get in, Isaura, unhinged by jealousy, can go out to meet them. Let's wait for her to leave her physical body during sleep and you'll see what I mean."

About two hours later, we saw Mr. Silva standing at the door waving to us from outside his physical body. Sidonio asked one of his assistants to take him on an educational field trip.

Brother Silva stated downheartedly:

"I wish Isaura would come along, but she just won't listen to me."

"Just let her be!" Sidonio replied very emphatically. "She's still not ready to heed our lessons."

Mr. Silva's face displayed profound sadness but he did not hesitate to go with his guide.

A few minutes later, Dona Isaura appeared outside her body. Her perispirit was extremely dark. She went right by us without paying the least attention to us. She had just one thought on her mind. Sidonio tried to say a few kind words to her but they fell on completely deaf ears. He also tried to touch her with his luminous hand but she hurried off on her unfortunate trip, leaving us to perceive that, at that moment, our nearness to her was true torment. She was incapable of registering our presence; nonetheless, she did instinctively pick up on our mental vibrations and showed that she was afraid of any spiritual contact with us.

Sidonio said that he could force her to listen to us, and thus oblige her to submit without reservation to our influence, but doing so would imply the undue suppression of any possibility for a learning experience. When it came right down to it, Isaura was the captain of her own destiny, and inwardly she had the right to make mistakes in order to learn from them. That was the best means for her to experience happiness. He was here to help her conserve her physical energies as much as possible, but he was not here to shackle her to attitudes that she could not yet willingly agree to, not even on behalf of the Good, which does not enlist slaves to spread it but free servants who are content and optimistic.

To my great surprise, Sidonio explained that Dona Isaura did in fact have a wonderful ability for serving others. But if she wanted to lose it for a while, we could do nothing but hand her over to the current of her own will until she herself could awaken on a higher plane of understanding. She knew good and well that her husband was not her exclusive property and that insane jealousy could only lead her to a perilous spiritual situation. She also knew that the Master exhorted his followers to forgive and love so that others who were unhappy would not fall into the abysses alongside the road. Nevertheless, if it was her will to linger on the pathway that was contrary to the one that the higher plane had laid out for her, we could only leave her circumscribed to the circles of a downcast or desperate mind so that time could teach her to reform herself.

After these patient explanations, Sidonio concluded with a melancholic smile:

"Education cannot be imposed. Each spirit has to decide whether to grow spiritually or fall deplorably."

We followed Dona Isaura as she left the house and went out onto the public street. She quickened her step until she came to an old, dilapidated and dark house. Inside were two discarnate evildoers, cunning enemies of the service of spiritual liberation to which she had become a devoted servant. It was obvious that they were hoping to poison her thoughts.

They approached her gently, unaware of our presence.

"Well, well, Dona Isaura," said one of the impostors in a deceitful voice of compassion, "your feelings as a woman have received a serious blow, haven't they?"

"Ah, my friend!" she exclaimed, obviously happy at having found someone who could empathize with her imaginary and childish suffering. "So, you too know what I'm going through?"

"Of course I do! I'm one of the spirits who are 'watching over' you, and I know that your husband has been your heartless tormenter. In order to 'help' you, I've been following that wretch everywhere he goes and I've seen how he has been cheating on you."

In tears, Dona Isaura confided in the false friend:

"Yes," she grieved, "you're so right! I'm suffering like crazy ... There's no one in the whole world who's more miserable than me."

"I know. I know the extent of your moral suffering. I've seen the sacrifices you've been making and I know that your husband prays at those Spiritist meetings merely to cover up his sins. A lot of times, while he's praying, his mind is full of lascivious thoughts about the women who frequent his home."

Enveloping the careless medium in his smooth talk, he remarked:

"That's just crazy! It really pains me to see you bound to a rascal pretending to be a disciple."

"Well, that's the way it is," confirmed the poor woman, as if she were a delicate swallow bearing an important message but suddenly caught in a vat of honey. "I'm surrounded by dishonest people. I've never suffered so much in my whole life!"

Nodding towards the sad scene, Sidonio informed me:

"More than anything else, the agents of disharmony are playing with her sentiments in order to destroy her potential as a missionary. Jealousy and selfishness are two gates of easy access to the overwhelming obsession against the Good. Due to her jealousy, she has linked herself mentally to the cunning enemies of her sublime commitments."

Displaying immense sadness, he added:

"Just watch!"

The cunning obsessor embraced Isaura and continued:

"Dona Isaura, you have to believe that we are your loyal friends. And true protectors are those, who, like us, know of your hidden suffering. It's just not right for you to have to put up with the deceitfulness of an unfaithful husband. Stop putting up with his retinue of hypocritical friends. They may seem to love group prayer meetings, but they are just useless clowns. It's dangerous for you to be involved in mediumship in the company of that kind of people … Be really careful!"

The careless medium's eyes opened wide in response to the strange inflection of what she heard; then she responded:

"Kind and generous spirit, you know how I have been suffering in silence. Please tell me what I should do!"

Bent on destroying the illuminative cell that was functioning with immense advantage in the home of the young woman besieged by his sugar-coated, poisonous arguments, the spirit remarked maliciously:

"Ma'am, you just weren't born for the circus. Don't let your home become a show ring. Your husband and his social acquaintances are exaggerating your faculties. You still need a lot more time to develop yourself sufficiently."

And enveloping her in the thick veil of doubt that annuls so many well-intentioned workers, he added:

"Have you ever thought about unconscious deceit? I mean, can you be sure that you're not actually deceiving people? You really have to be careful. If you study the serious matter of Spiritism intelligently and correctly, you will see that the messages you have psychographed and your incorporations of supposedly benevolent spirits are nothing more than the pale influences of troubled spirits, and a large percentage are merely the products of your own brain and your sensibility stirred up by the misguided demands of the people who frequent your house. Haven't you noticed that you are fully conscious during those so-called communications? Don't believe in abilities that you don't really have. Try to maintain the dignity of your home, because your husband has no other purpose in mind but to exploit your excessive gullibility and send you down the sad road of ridicule."

The poor woman – so naïve and yet so useful – registered that slant on the matter with visible horror.

Flabbergasted by Sidonio's passivity before such an assault, I asked him respectfully but far from calmly:

"Don't you think we should come to her rescue?"

Sidonio smiled in understanding and explained:

"Didn't we prepare her to defend herself just a few hours ago during the prayer service and with the fraternal help we offered? She worked as a medium with us; she listened to a wonderful, moving gospel talk regarding the perils of selfishness; she collaborated decidedly so that the Good could be concretized, and she herself lent us her voice so that we could teach principles of salvation in the name of Christ, to whom she must entrust herself; and yet, just because her husband was kind to a few women who needed his enlightening and fraternal company, her thoughts became darkened with jealousy and she lost her inner balance, handing herself defenselessly to spirits that exploit her sentimentality."

Sidonio nodded towards the discarnate malefactors and explained:

"Such low characters proceed with mediums like thieves, who, after plundering a house, awaken the owners, and then hypnotize and force them to take their place, compelling them to believe that they themselves are actually the thieves and deceivers. They approach the minds of careless mediums, wreak havoc on their inner harmony, upset their tranquility, and then, with imperceptible and subtle sarcasm, they force them to believe that they are deluded and despicable. A lot of missionaries let themselves be waylaid by the sort of false argumentation we have just heard, and they scorn the sublime opportunities to spread the Good through the invaluable sowing that would enrich their future."

"But isn't there anything we can do to get these evildoers out of the way?"

"Of course, there is. There is restraint and panacea everywhere, trying to fix situations by means of violence or artful 'diplomacy'; but regarding our endeavors, which would work better: shooing away the flies or healing the wound?"

He smiled enigmatically, and then said:

"Such difficulties are valuable lessons that, amongst incarnates and discarnates, the medium's spirit must take advantage of as invaluable experiences, and it is not our job to withhold the lesson from the pupil. As long as mediums are willing to listen to accounts that flatter them in their personal sphere, making it a condition for their taking part in the work of the Good, it means that they still value the phenomenon and the lower aspects of their individuality rather than their duties on the divine plane. In such a situation, they linger for a long time amongst idle discarnates who fight over the same prey, and consequently they nullify a priceless opportunity to grow spiritually, because after a certain amount of time in which they refuse help, they temporarily lose the edifying company of more highly evolved friends who futilely do everything they can to put them on the straight and narrow path again. Subsequently, they fall vibration-wise to the moral level appropriate for such a situation and cohabit with spirits whose company they prefer, only to wake up later and realize they have wasted precious time."

Meanwhile, Dona Isaura's obsessor was prattling on:

"Just study your own case. Talk to competent scientists. Read the latest news on psychoanalysis and don't waste the opportunity to live like you used to; otherwise, you could go crazy."

And he went on to say sacrilegiously:

"I'm speaking to you in the name of the Higher Realms and as a faithful friend."

"Yes … I can see that …" agreed the timid and downcast Isaura.

Just then, Sidonio approached the trio and made himself visible to the hypnotized Dona Isaura. She registered his presence with some difficulty and exclaimed:

"I can see Sidonio, our faithful spirit friend!"

Due to his low emotional pattern, the verbose obsessor was unable to perceive our presence, so he said mockingly:

"Oh, come now; you can't see anything! It's pure illusion. Give up this mental vice or suffer even greater imbalance."

Sidonio returned somewhat discouraged and told me:

"From the very moment that Isaura got involved in the dark realm of jealousy, her mind has been in a difficult situation and she is in no condition to understand what I tell her. Even so, maybe we can take a different approach to helping her."

We volitated speedily and found the medium's husband in an instructive meeting with several spirit friends. Sidonio told Mr. Silva to return to his physical body immediately in order to help his wife, who was in dire straits.

Brother Silva did not hesitate.

He rushed back to their bedroom and reentered his body.

Beside him, his wife's body was twitching in repeated contortions, gripped by her unspeakable nightmare.

Under Sidonio's kindly influence, he began waking her up by nudging her gently.

In copious tears, Isaura opened her fear-filled eyes.

"Oh! I'm so miserable! I am alone; all alone!"

Deeply influencing the complacent and kindly husband, Sidonio urged him to say something.

"My dear, remember our faith and how much we have received from our beloved spirit guides!"

"Oh, don't give me that nonsense!" she retorted angrily.

"What do you mean?" he replied patiently. "Haven't we been helped a lot through your own mediumship?"

"No! Not at all! It's all a farce. Those messages are just the fruit of my own imagination; all an expression of myself."

"Listen, Isaura! You've never been a liar. I can see you've fallen into the trap of our unfortunate brothers and they are leading you into a purgatory of jealousy. But Jesus will help us set things right again."

At this point, Sidonio turned to me to say:

"Andre, I think you have witnessed the point of the lesson. This is going to be a long, drawn-out conversation. With the miraculous concourse of time, we will pacify this respectable worker's exclusivist and careless mind. Go back to your work group and remember what you have learned here tonight."

Profoundly touched by what I had seen, I thanked Sidonio and left.

17
Fraternal Assistance

On the second day of the final phase of spiritual assistance for Margarida, our activity was crowned with sublime enthusiasm in the domestic sanctuary, which was finally draped with the gentle light of peace.

The place had been transformed.

Since the previous night, Saldanha and Leoncio had been the first to ask for something to do.

They were persistent in telling us that the enemies of the Good would be getting back to work. They were familiar with the cruelty of their former companions, and because many of Gregorio's minions would be checking to see if the alienating process of Gabriel's wife was proceeding as usual, Gubio began to implement a powerful boundary around the house and put responsibility for it in the hands of the collaborators that Sidonio had kindly lent us.

While we were working hard preparing defensive measures, Gabriel and Margarida were enjoying the happiness that had returned to their hearts.

Margarida felt lighter and well-disposed, and she gave thanks to the Eternal One for the "miracle" that had occurred. With the joy of a neophyte drunk on sublime hope, Gabriel was making a thousand promises involving spiritual work.

On our side, however, the responsibilities had started to grow.

In compliance with Gubio's orders, Saldanha went to another room in the house and, by indirect influence, urged an elderly incarnate housekeeper to dust the furniture, polish the decor and open the windows to let in vast currents of fresh air.

The home was filled with harmony once again.

The cleansing measures were going forward, when we heard harsh voices coming from the street.

Members of Gregorio's phalanx were shouting for Saldanha, who came to us looking downcast and somewhat troubled. Our Instructor suggested:

"Go, my friend, and show them you have taken a different path. Be brave and resist the poisonous fluid of anger. Be calm and diplomatic."

The look on Saldanha's face showed that he understood. He went out to face the troops.

One of them had a dreadful appearance. Hands on waist, he shouted irreverently:

"So! What's this? Disobeying your orders?"

Saldanha, now completely changed, replied humbly but firmly:

"My conscience has led me to make new commitments. I believe I have the right to choose my own course."

"Ah!" said the other sarcastically. "Now you have rights ... We shall see about that..."

Trying to impose himself more directly, he shouted:

"Let me in!"

"I can't. The house is under other orders now."

The other gave Saldanha a look of insufferable rebelliousness and asked loudly:

"Where's your head at?"

"Where is should be."

"Aren't you afraid of the consequences?"

"I don't have a thing to worry about."

The visitor grimaced in rage and stated:

"Gregorio shall hear of this."

He left with the others.

A few moments later, other elements assailed the entrance, desperate and insolent, but with the same results.

A number of scenes followed.

Gubio placed luminous signs in the windows, indicating the new position of that domestic shelter, opposing the spots of darkness that used to come from there. Suffering, persecuted but well-intentioned spirits were attracted by the signs and began appearing in large numbers.

The first spirit was a woman, who knelt at the door, begging:

"Benefactors from on High, you who have gathered in this house to serve the light, please free me from affliction! ... Have mercy on me! Have mercy!"

Our Instructor went to her right away and let her come in. On the side patio, she said in tears that she had been staying in a home nearby, where she was isolated by ruthless tormenters who were exploiting her vices. But now she was tired of her wrongs and yearned for a beneficent change. She was sorry. She longed for a different life, a different course. She was pleading for asylum and assistance.

Gubio consoled her and promised to help.

Next came two elderly men, begging for a place to stay. Both had discarnated as indigents in a hospital. They were filled with intense fear. They had not accepted the fact that they had died. They feared the unknown and pleaded for an explanation. They were on the brink of true madness.

An interesting woman appeared, asking for help against a large group of wicked spirits who were keeping her away from her son by inducing him to drunkenness.

Another woman requested protection against the evil thoughts of a vengeful spirit that was keeping her from praying.

The stream of sufferers was endless.

It seemed to me that Gubio's mission had suddenly become a huge endeavor of spiritual first-aid.

Dozens of discarnates imprisoned in the lower realms were now lining up outside Gabriel's house under the supervision of Gubio, who told them to wait for that night's prayer service.

And before the day had ended, several members of Gregorio's phalanx showed up, ready to take the road to renewal.

They had come from the colony we had visited. To my surprise, one of them was quite clear about what he wanted:

"Please, save me from the cruel judges! I can't stand the atrocities I'm forced to commit anymore. I've heard that Saldanha himself has been transformed. I can't persist in error any longer! I'm afraid that Gregorio will come after me, but even if I have to endure the most dreadful pain, I'll face it head-on. I would rather suffer his blows than go back. Please, help me! I yearn for a new course, one that will lead me to the Good."

We heard many such appeals.

As we lined up the well-intentioned sufferers in the large room, Gubio asked Eloi and me to make ourselves available to them, patiently hearing them out and assisting them when possible in order to prepare them mentally for the night's prayer service.

I must confess that I felt really at ease.

We divided everyone up into two separate groups.

I organized the brothers and sisters who were to be my responsibility into a fraternal group, but since more needy spirits continued to show up from time to time, I had to find more room.

Outside were many imbalanced spirits heartbreakingly clamoring to be let in; however, Gubio had stated that only those who showed that they were aware of what they needed were to be admitted.

Long ago I had learned that a greater pain always consoles a lesser pain and I limited myself to short phrases so that the poor spirits in my charge could comfort one another without the need for any counseling on my part.

Consequently, I asked one of the sisters, whose perispirit was in a deplorable condition, to describe her experience.

The poor thing grabbed everyone's attention because of her wound-covered countenance.

"Oh, I'm so miserable!" she began, "so wretched! Passion blinded and defeated me, and drove me to suicide! I was the mother of two children but I couldn't bear the loneliness that the world imposed on me when my husband died of tuberculosis. I shut my eyes to the obligations that were inviting me to an understanding and I refused to think about the future. I forgot about my home, my kids and my commitments, and I rushed headlong into the deep valley of unspeakable suffering. For exactly fifteen years I have roamed around without rest, like a thoughtless bird that destroys its own nest ... I was so foolish! When I found myself all alone and apparently destitute, I gave my poor kids to loving relatives and insanely took the poison that would do my poor body in. I thought I would either see my dear husband again or vanish in the abyss of non-existence. Needless to say, I found neither. I woke up in a dense fog of mud and ash, and no matter how loudly I cried out for help, I continued in unbearable torment. Covered with open sores, as if the lethal toxin had struck the finest tissues of my soul, I cried out aimlessly!"

She became so choked up with emotion that she could not go on. To press the lesson, I asked her:

"So you were never able to go back home?"

"Ah! Yes, I did get to, but as if to increase my anguish, when I touched my dear children, entrusted to close relatives, it caused them affliction and illness. The radiations from my suffering struck their frail bodies and poisoned them through their breathing. When I saw that my presence was inoculating them with a dreadful 'fluidic virus', I fled in horror. I would rather bear the punishment of my own lonely, aimless conscience than inflict them with undeserved suffering! I felt fear and horror of my own self. Ever since then, I have been wandering about without comfort or guidance. That's why I have come here begging for relief and safety. I'm simply worn out and beat."

"Well, you can rest assured that you will receive all you need by means of prayer," I explained, promising her Gubio's effective assistance.

The poor thing sat down, feeling much calmer. I noticed that one of the brothers present was seeking our attention so that he could reveal his own experience.

I examined him closely and saw that he had a weird glow in his eyes. He seemed crazed, smitten.

With the typical expression of chronic insanity, he began: "Can I ask you something?"

"Of course," I replied, a bit surprised.

"Tell me: what is thought?"

I was not expecting that sort of question at all, but concentrating my receptive capacity on giving him the right answer, I explained as best I could:

"Well, obviously, thought is our soul's creative power; hence, it is an extension of ourselves. Through thought we act on our environment, thereby establishing the pattern of our influence, whether good or bad."

"Ah!" exclaimed the odd gentleman, somewhat troubled, "that means that our exteriorized ideas create images that are as powerful as we want them to be?"

"Precisely."

"Then, what can we do to nullify our images when they wrongfully interfere with the mental lives of others?"

"Please, help us understand your case by telling us a bit about your experience," I replied with fraternal interest.

Probably touched by the tone of my kindly request, the man began to reveal his inner torment with hesitant sentences hot with sincerity and suffering:

"I was a man of letters, but was never been interested in the serious side of life. I cultivated a caustic wit along with a taste for eroticism, which I offered to the young people at the time. I didn't become famous, but more than I realized, I had a destructive influence on many young minds by filling them with dangerous thoughts. Ever since I died, I've been constantly hounded by the victims of my subtle insinuations – they won't leave me alone for a minute. And while that's going on, others come looking for me with orders and proposals entailing wrongful actions that I can't agree to. I realized that ever since my earthly existence I've been connected to a huge gang of perverse and mocking spirits that used me as a reckless tool for their undesirable manifestations. Actually, I had within my own mind enough frivolous and malicious material, which they largely exploited, thereby adding to my wrongs even greater wrongs, which they incited me to commit without my active cooperation. But now that I can see the truth, I have sought in vain to adapt to the nobler processes of life. Whenever I'm not beset by men and women complaining about having been harmed by my ideas on the physical plane, strange thought-forms confuse my inner world, as if they have become incrusted in my imagination. They seem like autonomous personalities that are visible only to me. They talk, gesture, accuse and laugh at me. I have no problem recognizing them. They are the living images of everything that my thought and my hand as a writer created to anesthetize the dignity of others. Now they attack, tease and flail me, as if they are children rebelling against a criminal father. I have been living aimlessly as a mental case that no one can understand. How can I comprehend these nightmares? Are we living dwellings for our thoughts, or are our thoughts points of support and manifestation for the good or bad spirits that are attuned to us?"

There was a significant expectation amongst the listeners, in spite of the overall calm.

The poor wretch said nothing more. Crazed and trembling, I could see that he was being tormented by energies outside his inner field. He gazed at me with eyes haggard with strange dread, and running into my arms he cried out:

"He comes one now! He's getting inside of me … One of the characters out of my raunchy writings. Woe is me! He's accusing me! He's laughing sarcastically and threatening me with his hands! He's going to strangle me!"

He put his hand to his throat and shouted in despair:

"I'm going to be murdered! Help! Help!"

The other troubled and suffering spirits were scared out of their minds.

Some tried to flee, but all I had to do was speak one sentence and order was restored.

The poor discarnate man of letters was writhing in my arms in such a way that I could not calm his depraved and wounded mind.

Cautiously, I sent a messenger to Gubio, who appeared shortly.

He examined the case and asked for Leoncio, Margarida's former hypnotizer. When he appeared, Gubio ordered him:

"You work on him. Give him some relief."

"Who? Me?" replied the half-sane convert, "I deserve the chance to provide some relief?"

Gubio replied without hesitation:

"Constructive service and destructive activity are both a matter of direction. The devastating torrent of water that destroys and kills can also run an electric plant. In fact, my friend, we are all debtors as long as we are on the side of evil. But we need to realize that the Good is the door to our redemption. The worst criminals can shorten years of punishment by working on behalf of others for their own rehabilitation."

To dispel Leoncio's doubts, he emphasized with a tone of kindness:

"Start today, here and now, with Christ. By being determined to help, you will find the secret to your own happiness."

Leoncio did not hesitate.

He began magnetizing the demented patient, who a few minutes later became silent and deeply restful.

From then on, Leoncio never left my side for the rest of the day. He carried out the functions of an excellent coworker.

The crowd was growing by the hour, however.

Well-meaning spirits came to us desirous of peace and enlightenment, but it honestly pained me to see such ignorance beyond the death of the body.

The vast majority of those present did not have the least notion about life in the spirit world. Their thoughts and sentiments were still bound to earth's soil. Anguished and disheartened, they were still connected to their old interests and passions.

Gubio was adamant as he issued his final instructions. That night would signal the end of our stay at Margarida's home and we had to prepare all the knowledge-starved spirits who were coming to us for the prayer service that he had planned. They ought not attend without having been advised of their new obligations and hopes.

Consequently, I took part in conversations, giving explanations as best I could.

At dusk, conformity and contentment reigned supreme on all faces. Our Instructor had promised to take the well-intentioned spirits to a higher sphere, assuring them of passage to better conditions. Sweet joy shone in everyone's eyes.

In the exaltation of the faith and trust that dominated us, a kindly woman asked for my permission to sing a gospel hymn, to which I happily agreed. It was wonderful to hear the beauty of the melody unleashed in notes of marvelous enchantment.

Joyful and comforted by the expression of service she offered us, my eyes were moist with tears. During the final verse of that song of hope, a young woman with a forlorn face approached me and said in a voice of supplication:

"My friend, from now on I shall follow a new course. In this setting of fraternity, I feel that evil will invariably drown us in darkness."

She looked at me with sad eyes, and after an emotion-filled paused, she asked:

"Please, promise me the blessing of forgetfulness in the 'realm of starting over'!"[17] I was the mother of two little ones, who were as beautiful and pure as two stars; unfortunately, death snatched me away from my home very early. But death was not the only torture to wound me ... It took just six months for my husband to forget many years of promises and he handed my two angels over to a spineless stepmother, who ruthlessly belittled them ... I have been fighting her with irrepressible revulsion for twenty months, but now I'm tired of the hatred that has constrained my heart! I need to renew myself for the Good so that I can be more useful. So, my friend, I am eager for forgetfulness. Please help me, for mercy's sake! Put me someplace where my bitter memories can die in peace. Don't leave me any longer in my degrading caprices. My longing for the Good is an insignificant vestige of light amid the darkness of the evil that envelops me. Have mercy and help me! I cannot yet love without violent and disparaging jealousy! Even so, I know that the Divine Master went to the cross in utmost self-denial! Please, don't let my lofty aspirations vanish!"

That woman's pleas and tears awakened the living memories of my own past.

I too had suffered immensely trying to detach myself from the inferior bonds of the flesh.[18] Highly touched, I saw

---

17 In the circles closest to the human experience, the "realm of starting over" means reincarnation. – Spirit Auth.

18 Read about Andre Luiz's own struggle in chapters 49, 50 of *Nosso Lar*, the first book of this series. (*Nosso Lar*, International Spiritist Council). – Tr.

her as a sister at heart and I took it upon myself to enlighten and assist her.

With tears in my eyes, I embraced her as if she were my daughter. Pondering the problems of all who undertake the revelatory journey of death without true love and understanding in their hearts for those they left behind, I exclaimed:

"Yes, I will do all I can to help you. Turn your gaze to Jesus and sweet forgetfulness of the troubled earthly realm will soothe your mind, preparing you for the flight to the towers of heaven. I shall be your friend and devoted brother."

She embraced me trustingly like a child who feels safe and happy.

18
Words of a Benefactor

The nighttime meeting held a joyful surprise for all of us.

In the soft moonlight, Gubio assumed direction of the endeavor and gathered us around himself in a large circle.

In his smallest gestures he was an invaluable guide who could take us to the peaks of mental heights.

He told us to forget about our former wrongs and he recommended that we foster an inner posture of sublimated hope framed with renewing optimism so that our noblest energies could be exteriorized. He explained that any matter of assistance, when guided by evangelical principles – as in Margarida's case – is always capable of bringing relief and illumination to many. Moreover, we were there to receive the blessing of the Higher Realms, but for that to happen, we had to hold to an unequaled position of moral superiority, because thought during such a meeting put individual forces in play of great importance for the success or failure of the undertaking.

Everyone's faces overflowed with contentment and confidence as our guide lifted up his voice and prayed humbly:

Lord Jesus, please bless us, your disciples thirsty for the living waters of the Heavenly Kingdom!

We are gathered here as willing learners in hopes of your sanctified determinations.

We know that you never hinder our access to the granaries of Divine Grace, and we also know that your light, like that of the sun, falls on both saint and sinner, the just and the unjust ... Even so, Lord, we have become atrophied because of our own carelessness. Our hearts have become arid from selfishness and our feet frozen in indifference, not knowing what pathway to take. Even so, O Master, more than the deafness that inflicts our ears, and more than the blindness that absorbs our sight, we suffer – due to our own wretchedness – extreme petrification in vanity and pride, which down through many centuries, we have chosen to be our guides in the abysses of darkness and death. And yet, we trust in You, whose sanctifying influence always regenerates and saves.

Powerful Friend, you who use fiery lava to open the bosom of the earth according to the will of the Supreme Father, free our spirits from the old prisons of the 'self,' even if it means our having to pass through the volcano of suffering! Do not relegate us to the abysses of the past. Disclose our future and incline our souls to the atmosphere of goodness and self-denial.

Within the deep night that we have created for ourselves because we have abused your blessings, we have only the flickering lantern of goodwill, but the winds of our passions may blow it out at any moment.

O Lord! Deliver us from the evil that we have accumulated in the sanctuary of our own souls! In your mercy, open to us the redemptive pathway that can make us worthy of your Divine

Compassion. Reveal to us your sovereign and merciful will so that, in doing it, we may someday reach the glory of true resurrection.

Far from the physical body for the time being, do not let us become like corpses in selfishness and discord.

Magnanimously send us the messengers of your Infinite Goodness so that we may abandon the sepulcher of our old illusions!

The serene tears of our guide received an immediate answer from heaven, because a veritable rain of diamond-like rays began to fall on him from on High, as if some mysterious and invisible power had unleashed a divine torrent of light on our behalf.

Gubio had finished praying, but the sublime sight elicited tears of indescribable emotion from all. There was not a single one of us that had not been visibly touched by the blessed ecstasy that suddenly emerged in our hearts.

The Instructor seemed to waver, in spite of the radiant aura that gloriously covered his venerable head.

He told me in a whisper:

"Andre, I need you to lead the work while I supply resources for the materialization of our benefactor Matilde. I see her here with us and she's telling me that the long-anticipated night for her maternal heart has finally arrived. Before her reunion with Gregorio, in the company of the blessed spirits who will assist her, she would like to visit us by materializing herself in order to encourage all those who want to apply for the preparatory work needed to enter higher spheres."

I quaked before such an order, but did not hesitate.

I took the wise Mentor's place while he took a few steps from us in deep concentration.

We saw a bright, soft light radiate from his chest, face and hands in successive waves. The light looked like highly tenuous starlight, because the radiations hovered in the air, as if forming singular pauses in his characteristic movements. In a few moments that soft, luminescent mass acquired defined contours, giving us the idea that invisible manipulators were infusing it with human life.

A few minutes later, the venerable and beautiful Matilde appeared before us.

The materialization of such a sublimated spirit right there had a profound effect on us. It was quite similar to what occurs in the physical sphere.

Several of the women, overcome with irrepressible emotion, prostrated themselves before the benefactor – a natural attitude that did not surprise us because we were, in fact, in direct contact with a glorious angel in female form.

The selfless Protector Spirit made a gesture of blessing, greeted us briefly and then spoke in a slow, emotional voice:

"My friends, all of you are waiting for the happy time of your blessed return to the 'sphere of starting over'; however, the gift of the vessel of flesh is a priceless divine blessing.

"Do not seek reincarnation only because of your longing for forgetfulness amid the dreams of the world, because temptations in the physical realm can become a real nightmare.

"The life that we know is a continuous perfecting process.

"Desiring to go back is not enough. You must direct that desire toward the Infinite Good."

She paused for a bit, and perhaps responding to the mental questioning of many of her listeners, she continued:

"Please, do not think that I am some special emissary from the kingdom of the light. I am just a humble servant with no other credit before the Eternal Giver except my willingness to help. My feet are still marked by a dark past, and my heart is still scarred from recent and profound experiences of bitterness that the unending days have not yet managed to erase.

"Therefore, do not entrust me with names and titles that are not mine. I am merely your sister in the struggle and I want to awaken you to the sublimity of the future.

"Our souls are temples built by the Lord so that he can dwell with us forever.

"Glorious seeds of divinity await our inner harmony and adjustment in order to sprout and carry us off to the resplendent realms.

"The soul's acquisition of illuminative virtues, however, is not something that happens overnight.

"We are like high-powered magnets or centers of intelligent life that attract forces that harmonize with our own and which make up our spiritual domicile. Wherever they may be, incarnate or discarnate individuals live amongst the higher or lower life rays they send out around themselves, much like the spider surrounded by its web or the swallow that zigzags through the sky on its own wings. All of us send out the energies we are clothed with and they define who we are much more than words can.

"What good would returning to the workshop of the flesh do if we do not understand our obligations before Divine Justice? Or what good would the temporary forgetfulness of the past – which is the strongest force capable of assisting us while in the circles of dense matter and which translates itself into a persistent noble tendency – do if we are not committed to righting our wrongs.

"The return to the physical garb is a blessing that we receive due to benevolent intercessions if we ourselves lack the merit to receive it when the time comes, much like getting a job in the corporeal realm with the help of friends, who guide us to the desired goal. Nevertheless, as often happens to many incarnates who hold respectable jobs, in spite of the fact that they do not deserve them, and who abuse the laws that govern our actions, many souls seek the sanctuary of the flesh making hasty promises and thus increasing their debts. Timid, frivolous or inconsequential, they use the blessed time in the Realm of Mist[19] to repeat the same wrongs as before and with a complete waste of the Lord's patrimony of time."

Matilde paused in her edifying and pious address to extend to us her hands, which sent out beams of intense light. Then she stated maternally:

"You pray to return to the protective veil of the flesh in order to undo the unpleasant marks on your perispirit. However, have you saved up enough power to forget the wrongs committed against you? Have you acknowledged your own wrongs to the point of accepting what is required to right them? Have you strengthened your spirit to examine your particular needs without maddening afflictions? Have you learned to serve with the Divine Lamb to the point of personal sacrifice on the cross of human incomprehension, annulling in your own soul the corrupted areas of attunement to the powers of darkness? Have you assisted your companions of the evolutionary and saving pathway with the intensity and efficiency that would justify your request for intercessory collaboration? What good deeds have you done to merit new resources from Heaven? Who can you count on so as to come out victorious in your upcoming experiences? Do you think a farmer can harvest a crop without having planted the seed? Have you stored up enough serenity and understanding in your hearts so that you do not poison yourselves tomorrow on the physical plane under the subtle bombardment of the dingy rays of anger, envy or jealousy? Are

---

19 The corporeal realm – Spirit Auth.

you convinced that no one can be warmed by the Divine Sun without first having opened their hearts to the currents of Light Eternal? Don't you know that you must also work to merit the blessing of a corporeal temple? Which friends have you helped so that you may ask for the love and sacrifice of fatherhood and motherhood on your behalf?

"Do not deceive yourselves.

"Only primitive individuals in the untamed spheres of nature are living semi-unconsciously because they are on the edge of the lower kingdoms. They receive reincarnation almost like animals, which perfect their instinct in order to enter the sanctuary of reason later on.

"For us, however, owners of strong minds, who have already lived within hundreds of diverse physical forms and who have already passed through many evolutionary climes, harming and being harmed, loving and hating, doing right and wrong, redeeming debts and piling up more, life cannot be regarded as a mere dream, as if reincarnation were a simple process of anesthesia for the soul.

"So, we have to remake ourselves completely, perfecting the vibrational tone of our conscience, broadening it for the supreme Good and illuminating it in the renewing light of the Divine Master.

"Honoring the heavenly gifts that have been bestowed upon it, the human mind cannot remain idle like a scraggly bush that produces nothing useful for the economy of the planet, nor must it be like the animal that remains behind in incomplete intelligence.

"For us, one human lifetime, no matter how humble it may be, is too important an event to be neglected. However, without embracing the notion of individual responsibility, which must mark our endeavor of sanctification, any undertaking of this order is risky, because, in our intensive process of learning and recapitulation, each spirit lives alone within the circle of its own thoughts. With rare exceptions, none of its companions along the way know about its noblest hopes or share in its dignifying aspirations. Each incarnate individual dwells alone within his or her own kingdom. A strong faith and much courage are indispensable for us to progress victoriously under the invisible redemptive cross that perfects our lives until the Calvary of our final resurrection."

Matilde took a lengthy pause in the address with which she enriched us during that time of wisdom and light. She approached Gubio, who was kneeling and looking extremely pale.

She thanked him kindly and then, as if she wanted to break the spell of solemnity that her presence had impressed on the gathering, she asked the audience for any comments they might make concerning their cherished plans for the future.

Voices of gratitude could be heard.

An intense looking gentleman was the first to speak:

"Great Benefactor, I murdered two people during my last incarnation. I lived many years in the corporeal body as if I were the most peaceable person in the whole world, despite a conscience fraught with remorse and hands stained with human blood. I fooled everyone around me with my mask of hypocrisy. Tormented by bitter memories, when I crossed the threshold of the grave I thought that dreadful accusations would be waiting for me. That idea brought me some relief because the criminal hounded by remorse finds true help in the humiliations that pierce his soul. However, I found only despair and self-loathing. My victims were nowhere to be found – they had forgiven me and had forgotten about me. Even so, I am persecuted by punishing forces that I couldn't begin to describe. There is an invisible tribunal in my conscience and I have futilely sought to flee from the places where I scorned my obligations towards my neighbor."

Suppressing his sobs, he finished:

"How can I begin the toil of my restoration?"

Such immense sadness was apparent in that humble voice that we all felt touched to the innermost fibers of our being.

Matilde replied without hesitation:

"There are other brothers and sisters nearby who are bearing the burden of the same guilt. They wander around, wretched, amid unspeakable nightmares and affliction. Open your heart to them. Start by helping them see the regenerative pathway and nourish them with hopes and new ideals, attracting them to the endeavor of sublimation through their own efforts by constantly practicing the Good. You will have to endure their insults, scorn and incomprehension, but you will find a means to help them effectively and kindly. After such sowing, you will begin to reap the blessings of peace and light because the spirit that teaches with love, even if it is criminally delinquent, ends up learning the hardest lessons of the responsibilities it takes on, transmitting to others saving revelations that are not its own. After you have accomplished such ennobling work, you will retake a physical body to recapitulate the lessons recorded in your renewal-interested mind. Once again, you will have to confront a thousand reasons to become violently angry and the temptation to eliminate your enemies with a deadly blow will visit you often. But if you can resist, and especially if you can defeat your destructive impulses when you find yourself involved with the blessed struggle in the 'sphere of starting over,' sowing love and peace, light and perfection all around you, then you will have demonstrated having made genuine and effective use of the gifts you received and you will have shown that you are ready for a higher ascent."

Before Matilde could put more luster on the lesson, a tearful woman sought her advice, exclaiming humbly:

"Great Messenger of the Good, I want to confess my wrongs right here in front of everybody. I'm asking you to please show me the way of regeneration. While I was incarnate, I was never punished for my excesses in the abuse of my senses. I had a home but I did not honor it, a husband whom I quickly left, and children whom I deliberately abandoned so I could indulge in the pleasures that youth could offer me. No one in my community had a clue about my moral transgression; but death decayed the mask that had kept me hidden from others and I began to feel a dreadful self-loathing. What can I do for a little peace-of-mind? How can I express the regret that fills my soul with infinite bitterness?"

Matilde looked at her compassionately and replied:

"Thousands of brothers and sisters who have shed their physical garb agonize in the next realm under the cruel gauntlet of the passions to which they so recklessly chained themselves. You can begin the readjustment of your energies by devoting yourself in the nearby circles to uplifting sufferers of good will. By denying yourself, you will pull many spirits from the quagmires of abuse. You will sow new principles and light in their minds, consoling and transforming them on the pathway of divine harmony. In return, you will have won the right to return to the blessed earthly school to perhaps receive the dire trial of physical beauty so that contact with the temptations of your lower nature can forge the steel of your character if you can remain faithful to sanctifying love. Such is the law, my child! To stand securely on our own two feet after having fallen into the abyss, it is imperative that we help others who have fallen into it, consolidating, in light of others' suffering, the notion of responsibility that must preside over our future actions so that reincarnation does not become just another immersion in selfishness. The only way for us to abandon wrongdoing once and for all is the constant support from the Infinite Good."

The benefactor paused briefly, looked out over her expectant audience and concluded:

"May none of us think that we have easy access to the eternal treasures just because we are presently free from the blessed chains of the physical body. God created imperishable, perfect laws so that we could not reach the Kingdom of Divine Light by chance, and no spirit can escape the wise imperatives of toil and time! Those who are planning to reap the happiness of the century to come must begin right now to sow peace and love."

Matilde finished, and while she seemed to be meditating in prayer, her illuminated chest area emitted spontaneous and shining waves of marvelous light.

19
An Invaluable Lesson

Obviously believing that she had given us a lesson that we could grasp, Matilde asked Eloi to bring Margarida to that loving gathering, indicating that she planned to solidify her equilibrium and strengthen her endurance.

A few minutes later, the object of our full attention over the past few days appeared in the room outside her dense envelope.

She was walking hesitantly and she seemed absent-minded due to her semi-conscious state.

From what I could tell, the lighting had no effect on her eyesight.

She seemed to be walking impulsively, as if she were an ordinary somnambulist.

She automatically fell into Matilde's maternal and loving arms, and almost immediately she reacted favorably by gazing nervously at us. She seemed to be coming to little by little…

Matilde wanted to awaken a few important centers of Margarida's mental life and began applying passes to her brain, an operation that I did not understand as well as I would have liked. She applied magnetic passes to the conducting nerves of the organ responsible for the manifestation of thought, as well as along the entire sympathetic region. Later, Gubio explained that the natural state of the incarnate soul may be compared more or less to deep hypnosis or temporary anesthesia, to which the person's mind, for the purpose of evolution, growth and redemption in space and time, descends down through the slower vibrations that are typical of the lower planes.

It was obvious that metabolic phenomena were occurring within Margarida's perispiritual organization became she began expelling from her chest and hands dark gray vapor-like fluids that vanished in the vast sea of the surrounding air. Right after this "cleansing operation," the areas of the endocrine system began emitting diamond-like scintillations, like a constellation of capricious contours shining in the darkness of her perispirit, which till now had been opaque and ordinary.

Luminous waves flowed continuously from Matilde's chest area, and we all got the impression that Gubio's ward was receiving a veritable shower of divine essences.

At a certain point during this remarkable *awakening* process, the young woman opened her eyes wide and looked at us like an amazed child. At first she tried to withdraw out of fear, but noticing Matilde's gentle, illuminated face, she settled down, as if magnetized by indefinable love.

Matilde kissed her lovingly. Upon contact by those sublime lips, Margarida seemed touched in the innermost recesses of her being and embraced Matilde, displaying true eagerness for spiritual wholeness.

Appearing wild with tear-filled joy, she cried out:
"Mother! My dear mother!"

"Yes, my daughter, it is I. Love never dies! The union of souls transcends both time and death."

"Why did you forsake me?" asked Margarida, holding her close in a rapture of inexpressible bliss.

"I never did forsake you! The land of 'carnal mist' may at times seem to distance us from each other; even so, no darkness could ever keep us apart. Our aspirations and hopes are mixed together like points of light in the darkness of separation, like the stars that resemble shining beacons in the nighttime fog, reminding us of the infinite and of eternity."

At the loving sound of those words, the former obsessed woman seemed to awaken more and more on our plane.

With longing eyes fixed on her mother, as if magnetized by immeasurable love, she asked in tears:

"Dear mother, I'm just so worn out and unhappy!"

"Oh? Now that the real struggle has just begun?" Matilde asked with a smile.

"I feel that I'm surrounded by heartless enemies. I'm being tormented day and night. I feel an invincible animosity between my sentiments and the world outside of me. Even marriage, in which I had put all my dearest dreams, has only been a dark book of cruel disappointments. My soul is overwrought and oppressed. Frustration and spiritual ruin are at my heels ... I know I've been a heavy burden to my devoted husband. He deserves a better fate."

Violent sobs kept her from continuing.

The venerable emissary wiped her tears and replied kindly:

"Margarida, living in the physical body while understanding our divine responsibilities is not at all easy when compared to the infinite glory that awaits us. We all have past lives of guilt to redeem; but we have to realize that if the human experience can be a dolorous path of personal self-sacrifice, it is also a blessed school in which the willing spirit can reach great heights. To do so, however, we must open our hearts to the inner climate of goodness and understanding. We are diamonds in the rough, covered by the hard gravel of our age-old imperfections, yet placed by the Lord's magnanimity in the setting of the earth. Suffering, obstacles and conflict are the blessed tools that cut and polish us. What would we say about the precious stone that fled the hands of the stonecutter, or of the clay that rejected the work of the potter? You have to change your attitude toward your enemies. Enemies are not always those who consciously practice evil. Most of the time, they just lack precise understanding. They proceed along a certain line of thought because they believe in the infallible pathway before their eyes. Like us, they face problems with their vision that only time and personal effort to do the Good can finally correct. Amphibians and birds are characterized by different impulses, despite being children of the same world. Margarida, we just have to know how to use our enemies as our instructors. Strictly speaking, due to our relatively unevolved position in the less elevated realm in which we live at present, we are natural enemies of the deeds of the angels. Nonetheless, the angels do not punish us for our temporary inability to understand their divine work in the economy of the universe. Instead of condemning us, they look with compassion on our deficiencies and extend their fraternal arms to us with a thousand invisible and indirect resources so that we may learn to scale the mount of sublimation on our way to the heavenly heights."

When Matilde paused, the young woman interrupted enthusiastically:

"Dear mother! I wish I could listen to the sweet music of your words forever! I'm so sad at foreseeing the whirlwind of earthly problems waiting for me. For now, everything is consolation and hope, but tomorrow I'll be imprisoned in the flesh once again and my memory will be anesthetized in a ceaseless battle with the monsters that assail me."

"That, my daughter, is the imperative of the task you're called on to do. Even so, don't waste the treasure of time on futile considerations. Fill your hours of wholesome work with all the harmony possible, the source of all beauty. The intelligence that has more or less gone beyond the limitations of animality finds itself in the physical body as a warrior in a stadium of beneficent trials. In the arena of the sublime possibilities that the realm of the fog offers, there are those who ascend and there are those who descend. Don't avoid the valuable hurdles on the road to perfection, nor drink the lying elixir of illusion that is so eagerly drunk by all who have been defeated by the temptations of discouragement because they were unable to accept the challenge that the world issued them. For every soul that triumphs on the thorny path, life is service, activity, ascension. And regarding the gale of struggles that will take you to luminous pinnacles, do not think you are all by yourself. Thousands of others sweat and bleed in silence. They go through life without the love of a spouse or the blessing of a home. Unlike you, they do not know the gift of a normal body, nor can they hope for the smallest dreams that you hold in your heart as a woman. They are forgotten men and helpless women who go from cradle to grave unnoticed and crestfallen. They live a regime of mental torment and they travel the road unprotected and torn as far as the world is concerned, stifling their sobs, which, if heard, would bring them implacable punishment. Nonetheless, in spite of the thick veil of tears that makes progress so hard, they press on fearlessly, believing in a tomorrow that is ever more imprecise and distant, and which seems to lie hidden on the endless horizon."

Lovingly following her mother's line of thought, Margarida replied:

"Mother, dear, please teach me to get on with my life. I want to honor the blessed opportunity I've received!"

"Do not try to satisfy all your desires. Instead, fraternally serve all who need to be upheld by a strong arm.

"Help others instead of seeking help for yourself.

"Understand others without expecting to be understood.

"Forgive others without asking for your own forgiveness.

"Support others without expecting to be supported.

"Give without meaning to receive in turn.

"Do not look for human respect, which can make you seem better than you really are; instead, in every time and place, seek the divine blessing of the approval of your own conscience.

"Do not seek to stand out; above all, perfect your own sentiments more and more without flaunting your vacillating and doubtful virtues.

"Act rightly and ignore the meaningless or poisonous comments of inveterate gossip.

"When receiving advice from others, distrust words that flatter your supposed personal superiority or words that could make you hardhearted.

"When faced with abundance or scarcity, remember the endeavor the Lord has called you to perform, and do good in his name wherever you may be.

"Remember that life in the physical body is extremely short and that your mind should always be filled with as many sanctifying ideas as your hands are filled with wholesome labor.

"But in order to carry out such a plan, you must open your heart to the renewing sun of the Highest Good.

"If your soul is shut against your neighbor's happiness, you will never find your own.

"The joy you spread around the feet of others will make you rich in joy.

"By sowing peace, you will reap your own.

"Such are the principles of the radiant life.

"No one can reap supreme joy by shutting oneself off from others.

"For the Divine Wisdom, the shepherd who has lost his flock is as unfortunate as the sheep that has lost its shepherd. Failing to assist others is as detrimental as losing one's way.

"Self-centeredness may create an oasis, but it will never construct a continent.

"Margarida, you must learn to go beyond yourself and heed the needs and pain of those around you."

The Benefactor paused. Feeling herself bathed in the infinite light of those unforgettable moments, Margarida asked, in heavenly bliss:

"O God! Most Merciful Father, to what do I owe the unforgettable grace of these moments?"

Still embracing her daughter and perhaps wanting to make the scene as familiar as possible, Matilde approached us and introduced us to Margarida as her personal friends.

We struck up a warm conversation that extinguished the wave of tears that had come upon us due to Matilde's moving and unforgettable lesson.

The time had come when the benefactor said she had to leave.

However, she first addressed her daughter resolutely:

"Margarida, now that you are as fully conscious of yourself in our realm of action as you can be, listen to us. Do not think that I have visited you for the mere pleasure of comforting you. That would perhaps lead you to the pathway of irresponsible unconcern, which never brings us true peace. In everything, the divine will has to be the soul of everything we do. The farmer who ploughs the soil and irrigates it waits for something in return from the crop that requires his daily effort. Whether direct or indirect, veiled or obvious, help from on High is not just a display of heavenly power. Those who live in the highest realms would never risk coming down to the home of the incarnate mind without lofty objectives, just as intelligent artists wound never, without educational purposes, influence spectacles of intellectual culture involving brothers and sisters whose reasoning and sentiments are still rudimentary. Time is precious, my daughter, and we can never abuse it without grave harm to ourselves."

In light of the questioning look on Margarida's troubled face, Matilde continued:

"In just a few years, I will return to the physical sphere of struggle."

"You will?!" cried Margarida in shock at the perspective of reincarnation for the illuminated being that had stooped to visit us. "Why would such punishment be imposed on you?"

"Don't hold on to such incomprehension regarding the law of labor," replied the messenger with a smile. "Reincarnation is not always just a simple regenerative process, although most of the time it does comprise a corrective measure for spirits that are obdurate in lawlessness and crime. The earth is like an immense ocean where the industrious soul finds eternal worth by accepting the imperatives of labor that Divine Goodness offers it. Furthermore, we all have sweet ties of the heart that may linger for many centuries in the depths of the abyss. It is crucial that we search for the lost pearls so that paradise does not remain empty of beauty to our eyes. After God, love is the glorious power that feeds life and moves worlds."

Matilde gazed at the rapt Margarida, and after a short pause, she said:

"In light of all of this, I hope you will not forget the wholesomeness of motherhood in the guidance of reincarnating spirits. Our highest potential might get lost in the 'sphere of starting over' due to the lack of determined and conscientious hands that could guide us through the labyrinths of the world. Love is almost never lacking in the home, where the soul adapts to the recapitulation of the important endeavor; however, limitless love can be as noxious as limitless harshness. Keep in mind, my dear, that when it retakes the physical body, the most ennobled spirit must endure the body's rules. The physiological laws that govern life on earth make no exceptions. They apply as strictly to the righteous as to the unrighteous. Of course, the angel who descends to the depths of the coal mine is still an angel, but it cannot escape the oppressive climate of the subsoil. Temporary forgetfulness will accompany me in the dampers of the physical cells, but the success I'm seeking will only come about if I can count on your strong and watchful guidance.

"I am well aware of the fact that when you retake the physical body that links you to the daily realm of the earthly struggle you will forget our conversation tonight. Still, the health and harmony that are going to flood your pathway from now on, along with the optimism and hope that will persist in your mind due to the indelible and vague memories of these divine moments, will not let you forget all of it.

"Care for your body, as someone who is preserving a sacred vessel for the Lord's service. You can expect me shortly.

"We shall live together on the meritorious pilgrimage.

"In the blessed kinship of blood, we shall be mother and daughter so as to learn more intensely the science of universal love.

"In fact, Margarida, my return is going to be a painful sacrifice for your fragile and delicate body; even so, please help me in the renewed sowing so that I may be useful to you in the inevitable harvest.

"Do not receive me in your arms as if I were a spoiled and idle doll. Outward adornments never bring the heart true happiness. Instead, a crystalline and edifying character is the only sure foundation upon which to build a good conscience. The greenhouse can nourish the prettiest flowers on earth, but it cannot produce the best fruits. The fruitful tree requires the constant care and assistance of the orchardman, but one must realize that it will only grow strong under the tormenting temperatures of high summer, hard rains and the gusts of the gale. Struggle and strife are sublime blessings, through which we can overcome our old obstacles. We mustn't belittle them but see them as blessed opportunities for our evolution.

"Please, understand my needs so that I can understand yours when the time comes. Human conveniences are respectable, but spiritual conveniences are divine. Help me to achieve stability in the former so that I may meet the heavenly imperatives of the eternal spirit. As soon as I am in your arms, do not relegate me to gaudiness and uselessness under the pretext of keeping me in your maternal protection. It is not with outward ornaments that we will enable the precious tree to grow and bear fruit, but with the persevering toil of the hoe, constant watchfulness, fertilizer and pruning. Do not lose sight of me, so that love for God and gratitude towards him may last forever in my fragile memory. Help me so that I may be useful when the time comes."

Edified by her indirect lesson, we could see that the tearful Margarida was promising everything asked of her.

What she had said applied to all of us and we would keep it in mind for a long time to come; however, we could see that Matilde was ready to leave.

She said a few more comforting words to her beloved daughter, lovingly applied magnetic passes to her to readjust her perispiritual centers, and then asked Eloi for his help in taking her back to her physical body.

Finally bidding us all farewell, the great mentor added a few parting suggestions.

"Margarida, do not forget the kingdom of beauty that you can establish in your home.

"Resolutely avoid the perilous ghosts of jealousy and discord. Learn self-denial regarding the tiniest matters so that you may happily receive the light that emanates from sacrifice. Do not use trifles to compromise the spiritual success that experience can offer you. You may now be free of outward evils but you are not yet free of your own. Trust in the Divine Power and don't lose heart, even when the tempest whips the innermost fibers of your soul."

Mother and daughter exchanged an embrace full of indefinable love, and approaching Gubio, Matilde discreetly explained the work she had planned for the next few hours, stating that she would be waiting for us nearby.

Then, she thanked us with exceeding kindness. She did not give us the chance to tell her about the acknowledgement and joy in our souls.

Matilde left after restoring to our Instructor the energy she had temporarily borrowed from him.

Gubio took the reins of the endeavor and informed us that, except for the four spirits who would keep fraternal watch over Gabriel's home, we should all leave for the higher spheres, stopping only in one of the "fields of exit" from the corporeal realm.

20
Rendezvous

It was getting late at night. Our Instructor looked around, seeming to consult the landscape outside in a brooding, pensive mood.

He gazed lovingly at his spiritual daughter, who was now convalescing in safe, gentle repose. He prayed for a long time at her side and then told us it was time to go.

Like birds returning to the nest of peace and hope, we now had to carry other wounded birds threatened by the tormenting passions. All the souls who had been helped there were to leave with us for other arenas of regenerative, redemptive activity.

Even the suffering, kindly spirits who were on the edge of madness due to the imbalance of their sentiments had tears of joy and gratitude in their eyes. In each one beat the yearning for rectification and new life. Perhaps, that is why they cast a troubled yet joyous look at our guide, as if they were devouring his words.

"As long as they are firm in their purpose of self-restoration," stated Gubio paternally, "all those who have been incorporated into our mission here will have access to circles of worthwhile work. There, students of the Good and of the light will welcome their aspiring to a better life. But I hope they are not expecting any miracles. The endeavor of readjustment is itself an article of the irrevocable law in every corner of the universe. No one should anticipate undeserved protection, or sweet-smelling flowers from the bitter seeds they sowed in the past. We are all living books regarding what we think and do, and the crystal clear eyes of Divine Justice are reading us at every moment. If there is a human ministry on earth that guides the lower life forms of the planet's soil, we too have the ministry of angels who direct our evolutionary pathways in our realms of action. No one can betray the established principles. We possess today what we gathered yesterday and we will possess tomorrow what we are gathering today. And since it is always harder to emend something than to do it right in the first place, we cannot rely with favoritism on the laborious endeavor of individual growth, nor can we expect a peaceable and immediate solution for problems that we spent many years weaving together. Prayer helps, hope soothes, faith upholds, enthusiasm reinvigorates and the ideal illuminates, but our own effort on the road to the Good is the soul of our hoped-for accomplishment. Consequently, even here the blessing of the minute, the gift of the hour and the treasure of daily opportunities should be utilized appropriately if we are aiming for a sanctifying ascent. Happiness, peace and joy do not happen by chance. They are acquisitions of the soul as it works incessantly to renew itself as it carries out the Divine Designs. Fortunately, since we are sheltered in the sanctuary of good will at this moment, we must not forget the gospel promise: 'Those who persevere to the end will be saved.' Without a doubt,

Heavenly Grace is a permanent, sublime sun. But it urges us to cultivate our higher qualities so that we can receive its rays."

During a brief pause, we became aware of the joy all around us.

A healthy optimism flooded every face.

Saldanha, with eyes glued on Gubio, amazed us with his abundant tears of purifying contrition.

Before our Instructor could continue the thread of his encouraging, vigilant discourse, a group of sisters began singing a hymn of praise to Christ's goodness. Their eyes used to be troubled and mournful, but they were now fearless, filling our hearts with unspeakable well-being.

Beams of sapphirine light were poured out abundantly over us as those harmonious, humble voices spread all around, touching the innermost fibers of our beings.

The melodious hymn reminded us of the sublime thoughts of the unforgettable Psalm of David.[20] When it ended, our Instructor explained that, in spite of the sanctifying joy of that moment, the battle was not yet over.

We still had to finish the epilog, he explained in a serious voice.

Matilde was waiting for us in an intermediate region, where the vibrational climate would enable her to materialize herself to everyone again to accomplish the long-dreamed-for rendezvous with her son of times past, and who would soon come looking for us to get revenge.

Displaying obvious concern in his lucid gaze, our guide explained that Gregorio was aware of the new developments in Margarida's drama, and was informed about the renewal of several of his colleagues and coworkers, now openly inclined

---

20 Psalm 90 – Spirit Auth.

to the Good and weary of ignorance, hatred, perversity and folly. Consequently, he had revolted against him – Gubio – and was about to come looking for him to settle accounts. He explained that a spiritual duel like the one about to be fought was going to require all of us to help with our prayers and mental emissions of pure love. We were not to view Gregorio's insults and affronts as personal offenses, or regard his attitude as the result of malice or unkindness. We were to see in his gestures of incomprehension the pain that had hardened his oppressed and rebellious spirit, and see in his words not deliberate malice but the outpouring of a sick and unhappy rebel who was harming no one but himself. Thought is a vigorous force that commands the tiniest impulses of the soul, and if we surrendered to its spiritual reaction armed with hatred or disharmony, we would be joining forces with violence and would impede not only Matilde's providential manifestation but the renewal of Gregorio, the entity whose intelligence was bent on evil. Emissions of bitterness or revenge would be counterproductive. Vibrations of fraternal love, like those bequeathed to us by Christ, are energies that actually dissolve the vengeance, persecution, disorder, pride and selfishness that torment the human experience. Furthermore, we were to remember that that mind, having strayed off the divine trail, was characterized much more by the disease of wounded and impenitent pride than by wickedness. Gregorio was merely an unfortunate wretch – just like we ourselves were in the near or far-off past – spurred on by inner rebelliousness and remorse that disarrayed his sentiments. Consequently, he deserved our loving and comforting dedication even if he seemed like a miscreant or lunatic. Moreover, such behavior should not be surprising, since, to teach us nothing else, Christ toiled on behalf of all yet suffered on the cross all alone.

Our Instructor added that when he came to us, the priest of the darkness would be accompanied by several companions that were as mentally poisoned as he was, and that in order to fight against that team of enemies of the light, we would have to form a fully harmonious defense with authentic fraternity, intercessory prayer and a spiritual love that feels compassion and acts in favor of restitution to the Good.

When Gubio paused, Saldanha asked him if it might not be better to at least organize a coordinated energetic repulsion defense, to which Gubio responded with a smile:

"Saldanha, in the company of the Master whom we embrace, there is only room for wholesome work involving an understanding of the lessons of sacrifice and illumination that he left us. One blow cannot be neutralized with another blow. We cannot heal one wound by causing an even worse one. Healing only occurs as the result of care, medicine and rehabilitation based on love. Those who plan on the Reign of Christ must surrender to Him. We are servants. Any defense depends on the Lord."

The former persecutor humbly said nothing more.

A few minutes later, somewhat subdued, we left the home where we had learned so many valuable lessons.

With the stronger ones helping the weaker, we cautiously set out on the road to the pre-established rendezvous site.

After two hours under the guidance of Gubio, who was fully trained for experiences of such nature, we finally arrived.

The area around us was strikingly beautiful.

A green plain crowned with moonlight invited us to meditation and prayer, and as if inciting our minds, the light, fresh breezes of dawn invited us to think comforting thoughts.

Our Instructor had us sit in a semicircle and recall various scenes from the gospels. With visible emotion, he told us that, according to a private message he had received, Gregorio and his cohorts were already headed our way, and that if any of us wanted to avoid him, trying to flee would be futile because most of the pilgrims gathered there were incapable of volitating to a higher plane due to the density of their mental pattern.

Thus, what we needed right now was the attitude of prayer and loving expectation of someone that was able to understand, help and forgive.

Precious stimuli fell upon us from the starry expanse.

Constellations shone in the distance, while the moon, silent and beautiful, seemed ready to witness our Christian effort.

I noticed that, seated on the grass, our Instructor had assumed the position of a mediumistic instrument, as had happened during the meeting, because he trustingly put me in charge of the group. I accepted without hesitation, although I was extremely concerned.

With such a measure in place, Gubio went into a heightened mental state through prayer.

We respectfully accompanied him. There was no place for conversations apart from the delicate issue of that hour.

We were waiting in expectant observation, when a far-off noise announced that things were about to change.

The Instructor, despite being pale himself, seemed like he was already in communication with high order spirits imperceptible to us, but after exhorting us to silence, patience, serenity and prayer, he asked up to watch everything that was about to happen, without revulsion, anguish or discouragement.

We did not have long to wait.

A few minutes later, Gregorio and a few dozen of his co-horts appeared, attacking us with harsh and violent swear words. They were accompanied by a large group of monstrous animals.

Under any other circumstances, we probably would have fled, had it not been for our Guide's wholesome warning. But

Gubio held his ground, resolute and imperturbable, sending out waves of intense light carrying imponderable magnetic energies, which came over us to strengthen us with the resources we would need for that irreprehensible procedure.

As I looked at the sinister faces approaching us, I must confess that I had never felt such fear yet such a contagion of confidence.

The priest of the darkness advanced toward Gubio like a general parleying with the enemy before beginning the battle.

"You miserable hypnotizer of naïve servants! Where are your weapons for our duel? You weren't satisfied with just wrecking my personal plans. You had to entice a number of my collaborators in the name of a Master who offered those who followed him nothing but sarcasm, suffering and crucifixion! Did you really think I would be willing to accept principles that undermine human dignity? Did you really think that I could be jinxed by the sorcerers of your lineage? You traitor of the given word, I shall destroy your bewitching powers! I do not believe in the sugar-coated love that you have chosen as your battle cry! I believe in the power that governs life and by which you shall kneel before me!"

Seeing that Gubio did not move, as if he were glued to the ground due to indefinable prostration, despite being surrounded by intense light, the priest of the black mysteries, stroking the handle of his gleaming sword, shouted angrily:

"Coward! Can't you stand up and hear my accusations? Have you lost your self-respect just like all those that have taken part in the movement of humiliation that has plagued the world for nearly two thousand years? Long ago, I too believed in heavenly protection through religious activity concerning the ideals you yourself now believe in, but I soon realized that the Divine Throne is too far away for us to concern ourselves with reaching it. There is no merciful God, only a directing Cause. That Cause is intelligence, not sentiment. So, I have shut myself off in that determinative power so as not to founder. The 'will,' the 'command,' and the 'power' are in my hands. If your magic can prevail over such principles, then accept the glove with which I slap your face! Let us duel!"

Gregorio cast a grim eye at Gubio's silent assistants and exclaimed:

"Here, at your side, lie helpless all my collaborators who have shamefully gone to sleep because of your alluring spell; however, every one of them shall pay dearly for their defection and treason!"

His cat-like eyes glared at us, but, except for me, who had to remain attentive to my duty, no one dared change the attitude of deep concentration on the purposes of humility and love to which we had been urged.

Displaying true disappointment in light of his unanswered insults, the fearsome head of the legions of darkness came closer to our serene Instructor and shouted:

"I'll stand you on your feet myself, using the blows you deserve!"

But before he could strike, a delicate luminous device in the form of a throat composed of radiant fluids appeared in the air. It resembled those that are formed during direct voice sessions involving incarnates. Matilde's crystal-clear, tender voice resounded above our heads exhorting Gregorio with loving firmness:

"Gregorio, do not harden your heart as the Lord calls you in a thousand ways to the work of redemption! The long period of hardness and barrenness is over. Do not fight against the blessed prodding of our Eternal Father! The thorn wounds as long as the fire does not consume it; the rock endures as long as the stream of water does not wear it away! For your soul, my son, the night that has eclipsed your mind in evil has ended. Ignorance can do much, but it is nothing when wisdom spreads its warnings. Do not think that the monsters of black magic can feed your heart with true happiness!"

The fearsome persecutor was confused, half-terrified, whereas those of us connected to Gubio's mission could not hide our immense surprise in light of that power-filled, unexpected scene.

I understood that Matilde was using Gubio's vital fluids to express herself on that plane just as she had a few hours before in Margarida's home.

The rebellious, bitter priest now had the look of a caged wild animal.

"Did you really think that love could change over time?" continued the sweet, motherly voice. "Did you really think that I could forget you? Did you forget the magnetization of our destinies? Even if my soul were to journey across a thousand worlds, I would continue to long for our spirits to be together. Thus, sublime light of love that burns in our deepest sentiments can shine in infernal abysses, attracting to the Lord those we love. Gregorio, arise!"

And with an inflection of tears that would disarm the most hardened mind, she emphasized:

"Remember who you are! Have you let the love we pledged to each other long ago in Tuscany and Lombardi die? Have you forgotten our vows at the feet of humble altars? Have you forgotten the crosses of stone that used to listen to our prayers? Did we not both promise to work together for the purification of the sanctuaries of God on earth? Always a fine and wonderful combatant in venal human politics, you let your mind become hardened by the madness of pride and vanity from contact with a perishable crown. You drowned precious ideas in the river of worldly wealth and you lost sight of the divine horizons by immersing yourself in the darkness in order to extend the realm of your caprices. You flattered the grandeur of the powerful to the detriment of the humble; you encouraged spiritual tyranny, believing you possessed infallible authority; and you believed that after death heaven was nothing more than a mere copy of the tribunals and courts of earth. But overwhelming disappointment surprised you upon awakening in the spirit world, and although humiliated and suffering, you coagulated your thoughts in the poisonous acid of rebellion and you chose the enslavement of inferior intelligences as the only position worthy of winning. For centuries now you have been only a harsh discipliner of criminal and perturbed souls that the grave caught in recklessness and vice. Has the sad condition of being a despicable spirit not pained you, my son? Such a question cannot go unanswered. The immense weariness of evil and profound inner loneliness that fills your time speaks for itself. You have learned with infinite disappointment that divine treasures do not lie in cold coffers of accumulated wealth, and you now know that Jesus has little time to frequent elaborate yet respectable basilicas, because from the dark human pathway emerge tears of pilgrims without light or home, without strength or bread."

One could see that Matilde, nearly choked with emotion, was finding it very hard to continue, but after a long pause that no one dared interrupt, she continued.

"How could you have thrown away for a few days of ephemeral authority our redemptive visions of Christ suffering on the cross? You have followed the Dragons of Evil for the mere idea that a temporary diadem could never crown your head in the realms of the life eternal to which death has brought us; even so, the Divine Friend has never decried our promises of service and he waits for us with the same selflessness as in the beginning. Let us press forward! I am Matilde, soul of your soul, who once adopted you as my dear son, and whom you loved as your devoted spiritual mother."

The messenger's voice went silent, interrupted by a stream of tears.

Doing all he could to remain standing, Gregorio cried out as if anxious to run from himself.

"I do not believe! I do not believe! I am alone! I have consecrated myself to the service of the darkness and I have no other commitments!"

Gregorio's voice, now less haughty, overflowed with a tone of indescribable terror. He seemed ready to flee, obviously transformed. But before the ecstatic and silent gathering, he remained magnetized by the words of the Benefactor, who made herself heard, austere yet tender, beautiful yet terrible, as she dissected his conscience. He had the look of a wounded lion, and finding that he was in the middle of all those who were watching the unexpected scene in astonishment, he displayed all the extreme despair he was harboring in his soul. He drew his sword and shouted in rage:

"I came to fight, not to argue! I do not fear spells. I am a leader and cannot waste time on useless talk. I do not believe my spiritual mother from times past is really here. I know all about the wiles of tricksters and I have no other choice but to fight."

Gazing at the delicate form of light hovering in the air, he added:

"Whoever you are! Angel or demon, show yourself and fight! Do you accept my challenge?"

"Yes, I do ..." answered Matilde with love and humility.

"Where's your sword?!"

"You shall see it presently ..."

After a few moments of anxious expectation, the luminous throat vanished, but a light, shapeless mass appeared nearby.

I understood that the valorous emissary was about to materialize herself right there by using Gubio's vital fluids.

Joy and amazement dominated the gathering.

In a few instants, Matilde appeared with her face veiled with highly tenuous gauze. Her shining white robe on her slender, noble frame under a sapphire-blue halo reminded me of some enchanting *Madonna* from the Middle Ages that had suddenly come to life.

Stately and calm, Matilde strode toward the somber persecutor; however, the perturbed and impatient Gregorio attacked her sword in hand, exclaiming resolutely:

"To arms! To arms!

Matilde stood still, serene and humble, though powerful and beautiful, with the majesty of a queen crowned by the sun.

A few moments later, she advanced, and holding her right hand to her heart, she stated in a gentle, loving voice:

"I have no other sword than the love with which I have always loved you!"

She suddenly unveiled her face to reveal herself in a flood of intense light. Contemplating her soft and sublime beauty bathed in tears, and feeling the loving radiations from her welcoming arms, Gregorio dropped his sword and went to his knees, crying out:

"Mother! My dear mother! My dear mother!"

Matilde embraced him and exclaimed:

"My son! My dear son! May God bless you! I want you now more than ever!"

That embrace entailed a frightful clash between the light and the darkness, and the darkness could not endure...

As if smitten in the corners of his soul, Gregorio had regressed to child-like fragility in a full swoon from the power that upheld him. At last, his liberation had begun.

The rapt benefactor held him in her arms as several members of the dark phalanx fled in terror.

Victorious, Matilde thanked us with words that moved the most recondite fibers of our being. Then, she entrusted her defeated son into our care, assuring us that the selfless Gubio would be in charge of her divine treasure for some time to come.

After embracing us affectionately, she dematerialized to our chorus of hosannas to prepare for the glorious future.

When Gubio had recovered, he rejoined us.

Edified and happy, Gubio supported the immobile Gregorio with his arms like the faithful Christian who is proud to support his unfortunate friend. He prayed surrounded by a sanctifying light, causing us irrepressible tears of joy and recognition. Then, amid triumphant and blissful peace, Gubio said our task had ended and that he was ready to lead the heterogeneous but expressive group of new learners of the Good, who had been gathered during the endeavor of saving Margarida, to an important and blessed colony of regenerative service.

**

It was time for me to leave.

My eyes were wet with tears.

The Instructor embraced me, and holding me close, said kindly:

"May Jesus reward you, my son, for your role on this journey of liberation. May you never forget that love conquers all hatred and that good vanquishes all evil."

I wanted to tell Gubio that it was I, an incapable disciple, who should be thankful; however, my voice was choked with emotion.

Gubio read the deepest sentiments in my eyes, smiled and left.

Eloi also left in search of other arenas of endeavor.

Returning alone to my spirit home, I prayed in tears:

"Master of Infinite Goodness, do not forsake me! Sustain me in my insufficiency as an imperfect and unfaithful servant!"

Unfathomable, sublime silence reigned all around me. But while the horizon was tainted with red, announcing the festival of the dawn, the Morning Star shone, twinkling before my eyes like heaven's answer of light.